Winners
Ethnic Minorities i ation

Winners and Losers:
Ethnic Minorities in Sport and Recreation

Gajendra K. Verma and Douglas S. Darby

 The Falmer Press

(A member of the Taylor & Francis Group)
London • Washington, D.C.

UK The Falmer Press, 4 John Street, London WC1N 2ET
USA The Falmer Press, Taylor & Francis Inc., 1900 Frost Road, Suite 101, Bristol, PA 19007

First published in 1994

A catalogue record for this book is available from the British Library

Library of Congress Cataloging-in-Publication Data are available on request

ISBN 0 7507 0342 3 cased
ISBN 0 7507 0343 1 paper

Jacket design by Caroline Archer

Typeset in 10/12pt Caledonia by
Graphicraft Typesetters Ltd., Hong Kong.

Printed in Great Britain by Burgess Science Press, Basingstoke on paper which has a specified pH value on final paper manufacture of not less than 7.5 and is therefore 'acid free'.

Contents

List of Tables

Acknowledgments

It is always an occasion of genuine pleasure for authors to express our thanks to those who make our work possible. First among those must be the Sports Council who, by its generous grant aid, made the research possible. No research is possible without funding, from one source or another, and that, in itself, is an occasion for thanks, but the Sports Council was also generous in the encouragement and practical assistance it afforded by making its own resources open to us and through the cooperation of its officers at all levels.

Second we must thank the members of the Advisory Committee who helped, well beyond the call of duty, in the conduct of the study. They were: Professor Brian Rogers (Chairman) University of Manchester, Dr Petronella Breinberg, Director, British Caribbean Link Project, Manchester LEA, Mr Bob Carroll, The Centre for Physical Education, University of Manchester, Mr Jim Clarke, The Sports Council (resigned, 1991), Mr Paul Eccles, Equal Opportunities Commission, Manchester, Mr Mike Fitzjohn, The Sports Council, Mr Andrew Lyons, The Sports Council (1991), Mr Kevin Moore, The Sports Council, Mr Vas Patel, Commission for Racial Equality, Manchester, Mr Malcolm Tungatt, The Sports Council. Our thanks are also due to Andrew MacDonald who, as co-director of the research, shared in the responsibility for its successful conclusion as well as significantly contributing towards the statistical analyses. Also to Bob Carroll who was responsible for the review of previous literature which formed part of the original report to the Sports Council and for the many helpful suggestions for the improvement of the study.

We also welcome the opportunity to pay tribute to the members of the field team of researchers who were responsible for collecting data by administering questionnaires and conducting interviews. Some were involved from the start and continued to the end. A few had to resign because of personal or professional commitments during the study and were replaced by others. All were generous in their commitment to its success. They were: Mr John Antonio, Mrs Atia Azam, Ms Janice Bobb, Ms Angela Brivett, Ms Julia Buckley, Mr Yiu Man Chan, Ms Veronica Henry, Mrs Kausar Hussain, Mr Abdul Jabbar, Mrs Loretta Lawford, Ms Karen MacArthur, Mrs Jasu Patel, Mr Daljit Singh, Mrs Raj Kaur Singh.

We are also grateful for the cooperation of all the respondents who gave up their time to complete the questionnaires and give interviews. We would particularly wish to thank the ten local authorities of Greater Manchester for their cooperation in supplying documentation and to the many officers who were generous with their time and invariably friendly in their response to our search for knowledge.

Finally we thank our secretary, Ms Janet Grimshaw. Phrases like 'without her unstinting help and commitment the work could never have been completed' are common in these circumstances. On this occasion we can write them, knowing them to be perfectly true.

Gajendra K. Verma
Douglas S. Darby

Preface

Winners and Losers is based on a two-year research programme carried out in Greater Manchester. In some respects it is therefore an unquestionably British study. The organizations which form the institutional context — the Sports Council, local government, governing bodies of sport, the education service — are all those of the United Kingdom. We hope and believe, however, that elements of it have a more than local interest and value. In chapter 3 we write about the ethnic minority groups who participated in the study. We take various aspects of their cultures such as religion, social and family structures and seek to show how these combine to make each group distinctive and different from each other and from the majority white community.

A people's culture is an extraordinarily powerful force in their lives. It helps to define their personal as well as their group identities. It belongs to them but, at the same time, they belong to it. It is also a very durable force. An obvious example would be that of the Jews who have retained their sense of Jewishness through the centuries and in whichever country they have settled. The strength of the cultural resources they were able to draw on which made this possible is equally at the disposal of the South Asian and Chinese groups of whom we write.

Whilst it would be foolhardy to assert that these groups will retain their characteristics with the same determination as the Jews have retained theirs, it would be equally unwise to assume that they will dispose of them in a generation or two. Modes of thought and behaviour that are deeply rooted in a group's self-perception are not lightly to be discarded so that they can be replaced by socially more convenient alternatives. To wish that 'they' were like 'us' is as silly (but not as funny) as the song sung by Higgins in *My Fair Lady* when he plaintively asks 'Why can't a Woman be more like a Man?'

The strategies employed by the South Asian and Chinese groups in Greater Manchester to cope with the problems of living in what, to them, was an alien and often hostile environment, were not arrived at irrationally. They grew out of the cultures they brought with them. Had we been studying similar groups in, for example, the USA, we believe that their responses would have been similar.

A major theme in this book is the need for all those involved in the promotion and provision of sport and physical recreation to recognize that ethnic minority groups *are different* and that the difference has to be accepted, understood and respected. The institutional apparatus to encourage and enable participation may differ from time to time and from country to country. That does not matter.

What does matter is that providers and minority groups engage in genuine consultation, learn about each other, understand the motives which underlie each other's responses to developing situations, and recognize the limitations which define the boundaries of the possible for both sides. If this can be achieved, then not only will more people from ethnic minority groups be able to participate in activities which have enriched the lives of Western Europeans for most of this century, but a small step will have been taken towards a kinder, more generous society.

Chapter 1

Introduction

Introduction

In March 1988 the Sports Council published *Into the 90s: A Strategy for Sport, 1988–1993* (1988) which sought to lay down its broad strategies for discharging its responsibilities under its Charter. It identified two principal target groups: young people and women. Within these, it identified unemployed people, ethnic minority groups and people with disabilities as requiring particular attention. 'In all three cases', it observed of these latter groups, 'the needs of the market are not fully understood and further experiment and policy development will be required.'

In recent years there had been some evidence to suggest that Government had increasingly moved towards the view that sport and recreation could, and should, contribute towards its other major social policy goals. It seemed reasonable to conclude that the Sports Council might reasonably give a greater emphasis to the function of sport and recreation as agents in the development of a more cohesive society; the selective targeting of groups within society at large, particularly ethnic minorities; and the further development of positive action policies and practices towards groups suffering from multiple disadvantages — social, economic, educational and recreational.

At the same time it was easy to observe changes in the national economic strategy which was increasingly affecting traditional leisure provision. These changes were leading to an increasing emphasis on leisure provision as a marketable, and potentially profitable, consumer good. The mutually contradictory stances in the economic and social policies as outlined above gave rise to some concern.

Additionally, there was growing evidence to suggest that racism, far from becoming a weaker influence in Britain (and in Western Europe generally) remained endemic in society. As Airey and Brook (1986) reported:

> In 1984 we described a British society that was seen by more than 90 per cent of the adult population to be racially prejudiced against its black and Asian members. Two-thirds also believed that blacks and Asians were discriminated against in employment. More than a third classified themselves as racially prejudiced. To complete the pessimistic picture, we reported that over 40 per cent of the population believed that racial prejudice had become more widespread in Britain, and a similar proportion

believed that it would become more widespread still over the next five years.

Two years later, after a period in which racial incidents and reports of racial discrimination have received a great deal of media attention, we find the same pattern of attitudes. It remains true that 9 out of 10 people believe that there is prejudice against Asians and blacks. In fact the proportion believing that there is 'a lot' of prejudice against Asians has increased . . .

It also remains the case that just over a third of people admit to being racially prejudiced themselves.

Nor was sport excluded from this general observation. Cashmore (1982) writes feelingly of the experiences of black sportsmen:

Being made to feel excluded at school, made the object of racist taunts by spectators, cast in the role of outsider by team mates and provoked by competitors, accused of lacking courage, determination and effort by coaches, and denied the kinds of access open to white sportsmen of comparable proficiency, these are the kinds of experiences which determine, or at least strongly influence the black sportsman's outlook generally and his approach to sport specifically.

Although an exploration of overt racism and its effect on participation by people from ethnic minorities was not a major objective of the study — Cashmore and others had already established this connexion — racism, conscious or unconscious, personal or institutional, has affected the responses of all ethnic minority groups to British society.

In thinking of the best way to investigate the issues that affected participation by ethnic minorities in sport and physical recreation, we were influenced by the observation of Allison (1988) that:

Most studies utilize traditional survey research techniques and limit their dependent variables to measures of recreational participation and/or recreational activity preference. Although such research has resulted in the consistent findings that racial/ethnic differences exist in recreational participation patterns (e.g. types of activities), this research has not led to further understanding of the source and nature of those differences.

With this in mind, it was decided that the central objective of the research should be to explore, as far as was possible within the agreed resource constraints, the relationships between ethnicity, culture and gender on the one hand and participation in sport and recreation on the other. In the course of this exploration, it was hoped that data could be collected which would give some indications as to the relative significance of ethnicity, culture and gender in determining participation in sport by people from ethnic minority groups. It was also hoped that the influence of increasing maturity would form another variable whose significance could be assessed. It was also important to attempt to place sport and recreation within the context of leisure activities generally in the lives of ethnic minority groups. Finally, it was also assumed that data would indicate the degree to which some of the Sports Council's traditional partners were responding to the demands of a multi-ethnic society as exemplified by Greater Manchester. The value and significance of the data collected would be assessed in the light of existing, more generalized, knowledge of the ethnic minority groups.

By adopting this two-pronged approach, conclusions could be drawn which would go some way towards taking into account the complexity of the ethnic, cultural, religious and other factors which contribute towards people's behaviour without confusing these essentially intrinsic factors with those arising from conflict with the culture and expectations of the white majority. Furthermore, by electing to place sport and recreation within the broader context of the cultural and social norms of ethnic groups, it was anticipated that the data would avoid easy assumptions based on models of minority communities which assume that 'they' are lacking in interest, the will or the ability to participate.

A review was undertaken of previously published literature having to do with sport and ethnicity. For the sake of brevity, we reproduce some of the main findings here and for the benefit of readers who may wish to explore the matter in greater detail, a list of references appears at the end of the book.

There is surprisingly little data on ethnic group participation in sport. The large-scale surveys, such as *Social Trends*, although containing statistics on ethnic group composition of the population of the country, do not use ethnic group as a variable in their leisure section (*Social Trends*, 1989). In 1979 Kew pointed out that there had been a lack of research and analysis in the field of ethnic groups and their leisure and therefore it was important to focus on major issues to guide research (Kew, 1979). We can say with modest confidence that there have been few attempts to rectify the situation in the intervening period, and there is very little on the subject even now. It seems to be difficult to locate references to the sporting and leisure activities of ethnic minority groups other than Afro-Caribbean and Asian. Thus references to the Chinese community, for example, substantial though it is at 157,000 persons, are notably absent. This lack is the more surprising if one compares it to the amount of literature produced on multi-cultural and anti-racist education in the last ten years, and the fact that many local authorities have sought to cope with the ethnic minority issues and produce policies in the recreation and leisure fields as they have had to do in the education sphere. The lack of literature and research may result from either the optional nature of leisure as opposed to the compulsory nature of education, or the status of leisure in the lives of people, and its status as a field of research. However, the value of leisure in people's lives and to the community has grown in importance, judging by the growth of the leisure industries and the increase in provision of facilities by both local authorities and commercial organizations, whilst the volume of literature and research in leisure generally has grown tremendously in the last decade. There is clearly, then, a large gap which needs to be addressed and one of the major objectives of this research has been to help to fill that gap. The literature which does exist can be divided into a) participation surveys, b) physical education/sport at school level, c) community sport, and d) elite and professional sport.

Participation Surveys

The large-scale surveys have not used ethnic groups as a variable. One of the few that does mention ethnic groups is a DES survey of young people completed in 1981 and is now out of date (DES, 1983). Typically, ethnicity was defined in the following terms, 'Caucasian', 'West Indian' and 'Asian'. Such categorization indicates a minimal level of awareness of the complexity of ethnicity (Verma, 1986), and serves little purposes.

Ethnicity implies membership of a specified group which is distinctive in terms of certain characteristics; these might include language, religion, cultural values and lifestyles. Nevertheless, individuals are often arbitrarily assigned to particular categories on the basis of physical appearance. In the United States, for example, people with more Caucasian than Negro ancestry are nevertheless perceived as 'blacks'. It is ironical that a person who is 'black' in North America might be 'white' in Puerto Rico. In North American and European countries the term 'black' is occasionally used as a symbolic term to describe groups who, as a result of racialism and experience of colonialism of various types, have had a particular identity forced upon them. Indeed, in the UK, both Afro-Caribbeans and Asians (and sometimes Greeks and Turks) may classify themselves as 'blacks' to indicate their political orientation — not their ethnicity. In Britain the terms 'black' and 'Asian' are used to describe people of Caribbean, African and South Asian origin or ancestry.

A number of small-scale surveys have been undertaken which provided interesting participation patterns but could not be generalized because of the nature of the local provisions and policies, as well as the nature and size of the ethnic groups concerned. However, they did suggest that there were notable gender differences in participation, particularly for Muslims of South Asian origin.

Physical Education and Sport at School Level

Many writers have discussed the way that Afro-Caribbean youngsters have been systematically encouraged to make sport their prime concern. They have noted that success has undoubtedly had positive benefits in terms of the individual's self-concept but there has been general agreement that this has not been without a price. This has been defined as: the diverting of effort away from academic work, thus perpetuating the stereotype of Afro-Caribbeans as being physically but not intellectually gifted; the narrowing of post-school opportunities. Thus the efforts of many well-meaning and committed teachers, carried out in the name of 'equality of opportunity' and 'catering for the needs of individual children', have had the unlooked for consequence of reproducing the existing inequalities in society. Particularly noteworthy is the fact that, although the numbers of black athletes have risen significantly, few have been recruited into decision-making positions in their sport.

There is little mention of PE in the literature of multi-cultural and anti-racist education. In the PE literature, there are a few, short articles mentioning the 'problems' that arose and suggesting policies to overcome them and some LEAs responded by issuing guidelines to their schools. The emphasis has been on the ethnic group having a 'problem' and not on the possibility of institutional racism. Some writers have pointed out that schools with well-developed equal opportunities policies have been unable to achieve 'any significant increase in [South Asian] girls' participation and have suggested that such policies were unlikely to succeed unless they took into account their cultural traditions and religious beliefs. One study, taking this as its starting point, showed how, from the perspective of Islam, policies leading to equality of opportunity and the development of the individual, can be regarded as attacking fundamental values in cultural and religious traditions.

Community Sport

This literature deals mainly with local authority policies and reports of local schemes and much of it is hard to locate. What has been located invariably refers to Asian and Afro-Caribbean groups with all the over-simplification which that implies.

The largest concentrations of ethnic minority populations have been in the inner city areas and they have invariably been the areas of the worst social conditions, poorest housing, highest unemployment, and lack of facilities for sport and leisure. These types of conditions helped to provoke the riots in Brixton of 1981 followed by the Scarman Report (1982).

The Race Relations Act (1976) requires that people from ethnic minorities shall not be discriminated against in the provision of goods and services and makes positive action in their favour permissible. Perhaps because of the complexity of the problem, little has been done outside the education service in relation to the provision of services. However, it was the clear intention of the Act that services should be covered by its provisions and the existing attempts by the Sports Council makes it clear that it recognizes that ethnic minorities have been recreationally disadvantaged and that positive action is permissible in its attempts to rectify matters.

Even before Scarman, some local authorities had seen the need to combat racial disadvantage in the leisure services, such as in Bradford (King *et al.*, 1983).

What distinguished Bradford's approach from that of London or Manchester was its perception that its proper target was not the regeneration of its inner-city areas but adequate provision for its ethnic minority groups who lived in them. The Manningham sports facility in Bradford created in 1979 is an example of a community provision with the community views being considered and related to consumer demand. There was initially a policy of employing both experienced staff and staff from the ethnic group community. The acceptability of the facility to the community has become apparent, something which has not always happened elsewhere with local ethnic group communities, attested by the figures of over 60 per cent usage by the largely South Asian local community and the fact that the centre is even used as a Mosque and for Asian meetings.

Other commentators have shown that institutional racism is common in leisure services in Britain and that black people are normally excluded from the decision-making processes and positions of power. Where this pattern is broken, as in the Bradford experience, there is evidence to show that ethnic minority people will participate and use the leisure centres if the right approach is made and the management, staffing and activities reflect their needs.

Elite and Professional Sport

The largest body of literature is in the field of elite and professional sport, but it has the least relevance to the issue of the scale and nature of participation by ethnic minorities. The majority of the literature comes from America and applies to that society, although of course it does have international repercussions and application.

The main themes running through British studies, which also appear in the American literature, are these. Firstly, the condemnation of views such as those held by Kane (1971) who argued that the success of black athletes was attributable to their genetic inheritance leading to superior natural ability. Secondly, support to the view that success by black athletes was much more to do with their perception of sport as a way of achieving social and economic success in life. Thirdly, it emphasizes the lack of black people in decision-making and positions of power and authority in sport. This is supported by Ouseley (1983) and Miller (1985).

The influence which successful black sportsmen have on ordinary people's participation derives from their position as role models. Prominence in the media of black sportsmen is held by many to enhance the possibility of increased participation by black people. However, the effects of their disadvantage and social class needs to be extricated from the ethnicity factor if we are to get a real understanding of ethnic group participation, whilst a complete understanding of ethnic group culture, that is not just a Eurocentric model, needs to be tackled in the literature and appropriate research needs to become a reality to complete the picture.

With honourable exceptions, often small-scale studies of particular groups, previous literature has signally failed to differentiate between the various ethnic groups whose origins lay in the rich diversity of the Indian sub-continent. They have been lumped together as 'Asians' in complete disregard for their differences of language, religion, economic background, social customs, family structures, notions of propriety and morality, patterns of work and leisure habits. In this study, we have distinguished between Indians, Pakistanis, Bangladeshis and East African Asians and have attempted to portray their patterns of sport and physical recreation within the context of their leisure activities generally. A similar attempt has been made with the Chinese and African communities.

Chapter 2

Research Strategies and Tactics

In this chapter we briefly outline the general intentions which informed the nature of the research which led to this book. We also give an indication of the methods we employed to collect the data which form the basis of chapters 4 and 5.

In line with our intention to look at a range of factors having a bearing on the participation in any kind of sporting or physical activity by people from ethnic minority communities, we developed five broad categories which seemed to include those factors which might affect them. They were:

- Those peculiar to people from ethnic minorities whose cultural traditions were different from those of the white majority.
- Those factors which people from ethnic minorities shared with their white peers. These were perceived as being essentially related to age, gender, life cycle, class and socio-economic status; the culture of expectations; social skills and self-confidence.
- Racial and sexual discrimination by the providers of sporting and recreational facilities. Included in this are unconscious and institutional as well as overt and personal discrimination.
- Racial discrimination within society at large. The concern here was to identify whether, and if so, how the perceptions of people from ethnic minority communities about the accessibility of sporting and recreational facilities of whatever kind might be affected by a sense of threat from the white majority.
- Relevant legislation. We identified the possibility that compulsory competitive tendering (Local Government Act (2) 1988) and the Education Reform Act, 1988 (provisions relating to the Local Management of Schools) might have an impact on the intentions or practices of local authority providers which could significantly affect ethnic minority groups. Specifically, was it likely that the emphasis placed on getting value for money in local government and on schools as cost centres with a responsibility for generating some of their own income would lead to a decrease in provision for ethnic minority groups?

It seemed at least possible at the time that this legislation might well have unforeseen as well as desired consequences. Many of its provisions took as their starting point the notion of the population as 'consumers', which implied a contract between them and the providers to give value for money. In short, commercial considerations had been introduced in areas of public life where they had played no part in the past. The significance of this was not easily over-stated. Whereas before, local government and education had a duty to supply services which were perceived as being of implicit value to the local community, those services were now to be seen as commodities with a price. Put another way, it was the cost that was to drive the service. Thus, before we began our investigation, we were troubled by the thought that this new direction would result in increased pressures to supply benefits to those who could afford to pay for them. In the case of sport and leisure provision, little was discovered to allay those fears.

The Education Reform Act, 1988 was intended to change fundamentally the nature of the State school system and the education it provided. Earlier legislation had created a national system, administered through Local Education Authorities (LEAs) which were, in effect, the local authorities responsible also for a vast range of other local services. It was the duty of the LEAs to provide schools, staff them with teachers and equip them adequately for their purposes. Thus it was that headteachers and governing bodies of schools were very restricted in their ability to make any decisions with financial implications. They controlled quite trivial budgets — such as those for educational consumables for example — but practically all other decisions involving money were either made for them, or could only be made with the approval of, the LEA.

In contrast with their financial powerlessness, headteachers had almost unlimited discretion over the content and methods of delivery of the curriculum. There were pressures which ensured that excessive eccentricity in the nature of the education provided by a school was curbed. Parents, LEA advisers, Her Majesty's Inspectors and, for secondary schools, the need to prepare pupils for public examinations, all helped to ensure that there was a broad similarity between one school and another. But this broad similarity concealed wide variations in the balance of subjects taught, the emphasis placed on parts of the school's curriculum and the expectations teachers had of the pupils.

The Education Reform Act changed both the financial and the pedagogic assumptions. Headteachers and their governing bodies were largely freed from their financial dependency. They now had a duty to balance their school budgets and with that duty, powers to determine the number of teachers they could afford to employ as well as the opportunity to augment their budgets by making charges to local groups who wished to make use of the school's facilities. This new arrangement was described as Local Management of Schools (LMS). It effectively re-wrote the job descriptions of headteachers. Conversely, the Act introduced a National Curriculum which was to be followed by all schools and a system of testing which would chart the progress of all pupils. The results of the test were to be published so that parents could make objective comparisons between the performance of schools and so make informed decisions about where to send their children. Since school budgets were directly linked to the number of pupils on roll, it was clearly in the interest of schools for their pupils to perform well in the tests.

The changes that were to flow from the Education Reform Act were unclear at the time of the research and, so far as their impact on sport and physical education are concerned, still have to work their way through a system that is very resistant to change. Many active in the field were very troubled by the possible long-term effects both to the schools and the communities they served.

Six ethnic groups were originally selected to participate in the research. They were all to be found in substantial numbers in Greater Manchester and were: Afro-Caribbean, Bangladeshi, Chinese, East African Asian, Indian and Pakistani. These groups were selected for a number of reasons but chiefly because they shared the following characteristics. They were all of non-European origin; they were present not only in Greater Manchester but had a national distribution; and, they perceived themselves as forming communities having common attributes. Subsequently, a seventh group, those of African origin, was added. Finally, a white British group of similar socio-economic status was included in the sample in the hope that it would make some interesting comparisons possible.

Our study focused in the first instance on the attitudes (and the variations in attitude) of the various ethnic minority groups towards the development of their physical potential; whether, for instance, their cultural traditions led them to believe that it was a desirable end in itself and, if so, what made it desirable. The phrase 'cultural traditions' is used loosely here to embrace all those beliefs, practices, notions of propriety; inter-personal relationships; personal and familial ambitions; moral and religious imperatives; in fact, all those sets which are the result of social conditioning within the family and community and the experience of society at large which can substantially affect the pattern of ambition and behaviour. It attempted to establish the part played by activities supported by the Sports Council in achieving their objectives and to explore the possibility that certain minority groups might welcome support for activities that are outside the mainstream of Western European culture.

A second focus was on the factors peculiar to ethnic minority groups which might either inhibit or encourage participation. To this end, part of the study was devoted to an exploration of the effects of such constraints as: religious imperatives, the need for parental approval, peer group pressures, established customs and practices within the communities, the self-concept, and the sense of alienation from or integration with the majority community. Closely allied to this last is the perception by young people from ethnic minorities of local authority and commercially provided facilities as welcoming/neutral/unwelcoming institutions.

A third focus was on factors which might inhibit or encourage participation in sport or active leisure but which were not specific to ethnic minorities. Thus part of the study explored the impact of such matters as: economic constraints, ease of access to facilities, patterns of work, gender, life cycle and age. We were well aware of the power of social class as a determinant of behaviour. However, we also felt that enough was already known on this subject and to include it as a major consideration might well get in the way of what we were really interested in.

A fourth focus was on those factors which aided or encouraged young people from ethnic minorities to take an active part in sport and recreation. Within this we were concerned by the part played by direct advertising and promotions and the media generally in its role of creating lifestyles for young people. Such questions as the presence or absence of role models and their influence and the influence of senior members of the communities were also seen as significant.

It was anticipated that some ethnic groups might be sensitive, even resistant, to providing information, and that access to certain sections of the community would not be easy for both cultural and religious reasons. To take but one obvious example: a combination of gender and religious factors could prejudice acceptability of research workers to specific groups. For example, access to Muslim women would be difficult to achieve for a white male research worker, nor could she be expected to respond readily to him.

It was therefore thought desirable to make approaches to leaders or representatives of the ethnic communities identified for the research, in order to alert them to what was being planned and to seek their views, comments and possible help. It was also vital that the confidence of potential respondents was gained, and that the people who collected the information should be acceptable to them. This was particularly important since some of the information, at least, was expected to be collected through recorded interviews. It was clearly necessary to recruit a team of researchers who would be prepared and able to do the work in the field and who also shared the ethnic origins of the people with whom they were working. We were fortunate in being able to do this.

Research Strategies

The research strategies adopted grew out of the nature of the project. In the first place, the Sports Council was interested in five aspects which it had identified:

a)   The function of sport and recreation as agents in the development of a more cohesive society in the UK.

b)   The adoption of a proactive rather than a reactive stance by the Sports Council.

c)   A greater emphasis on the selective targeting of groups within society at large.

d)   A greater concentration of resources on the inner-city areas and, as a consequence of the above,

e)   The development of positive action policies and practices towards disadvantaged groups.

There was effectively no data available in the form and quantity required. The only way to generate it was by the development of a questionnaire which would meet the objectives of the research. We were very conscious, however, that satisfying as quantitative data is to the researcher, providing, as it does, opportunities for computer analysis and tables and graphs and all the paraphenalia that goes with writing a research report, it could not tell the whole story. However carefully constructed, the answers provided by a questionnaire supply information limited by the questions asked. To overcome this, we decided that we would ask one in ten of the people who completed the questionnaire to agree to a recorded interview.

We set a target of 100 males and 100 females in each of the major ethnic groups who participated in the study, covering the age range from school leavers to 30 year olds. Completed questionnaires were monitored as they came in to ensure they presented a balanced picture so far as ethnicity, age, gender, economic status and parenthood were concerned. Of these, we were well aware that the data on economic status was the least reliable. Our best safeguard came from the fact that the field researchers were of the same ethnic origin and lived within the community concerned. Part of their brief was to ensure, as far as they were able, that people they approached from their community reflected in its range and proportion the economic success of its members.

The questionnaire was designed for semi-assisted administration and fell into three major sections. The first was designed to elicit biographical details together with a self-ascribed ethnic origin, religious affiliation, and friendship patterns. It then moved to matter in relating to sport and recreation with questions on past and present participation, the nature of the facilities used and, where relevant, reasons for discontinuing participation in any activities. The third main section was concerned with discovering something about the respondent's perception of fitness in him/herself, reasons for desiring fitness, or not as the case might be, and responses to the media presentation of people playing games etc., as part of a desirable lifestyle. It also attempted to assess the importance of family, peer group and other influences on behaviour.

Data was recorded for up to six main activities in which the respondents might take, or have taken part, and questions then asked regarding:

- frequency of participation,
- who people took part with,
- ethnicity of group membership,
- location of activity,
- influences on participation.

Questions were also asked about what people might like to do and why they currently did not; whether they perceived any barriers to participation, and whether they had ever encountered opposition to participation.

We have already mentioned the importance we attached to data provided by the interviews. They were seen as an extension of the questionnaire and as an opportunity to probe for the causes, motives, feelings, perceptions, and responses which lay behind their involvement, or lack of it, in physical recreation. At the time of the interview, the interviewer had the completed questionnaire with him or her so that its contents could be used to lead the interviewee into a deeper explanation of his/her thoughts and experiences. It explored physical recreation within the general context of leisure time; school experiences and influences; motives for participation or avoidance; contact with other ethnic groups; experiences particularly relevant to women; experiences within recreation and more generally in society of racial prejudice; and thoughts on the behaviours of other ethnic groups.

While the bulk of the data on specific ethnic groups were produced by the questionnaires and interviews, experience of other research connected with ethnic minority groups had shown the wisdom of collecting information from sources other than the principal respondents. In the context of this research these were thought to include the local authorities who provided so many of the facilities for sport and recreation, and were concerned with such matters as the implementation of equal opportunity policies; the Sports Council which, through the regional structure, helped to coordinate many of the developments, services, and information currently in existence; the governing bodies of sport whose influence tended to be specific; local sports clubs whose activities, policies and provisions could be relevant to some members of the samples; and leaders of ethnic minority groups who might well have been aware of issues which would otherwise be easily overlooked.

The approach used to collect such information included semi-structured interviews conducted with representatives of the local authorities including leisure department personnel, Regional Sports Council officers, and community leaders. Governing bodies of sport were requested to provide written evidence of any policy documents with relevance to ethnic minority participation or procedures which they had adopted or were in the process of planning.

Chapter 3

Brief Portraits of the Ethnic Minority Communities

The purposes of the research were to discover something of the level of involvement by people of ethnic minority origin in sport and physical recreation, their preferred activities, and the factors which had a bearing on their participation. There were clearly two sides to the equation. On the one hand it was necessary to find out the extent to which providers were actively seeking to provide equal access to all and we have a good deal to say about that in chapter 4. On the other hand, there were the people themselves: people whose personal, national and ethnic histories were far removed from those of the white British majority. To understand their intellectual, emotional and social responses to the constant challenges posed by British society, it seemed that a little knowledge about them might provide a basis for intelligent empathy.

It was this that led us to put together a series of thumbnail sketches of the ethnic minority groups who featured in our study. We begin, however, by writing briefly about the national patterns of settlement.

The ethnic group of residents for Great Britain as a whole, and for its major regions, is given in Table 1. The figures are self-explanatory but at the risk of tedium, one or two obvious facts may be reinforced. First, ethnic minority groups in Great Britain are properly so called. As a proportion of the whole population, they are a small minority collectively. Taken severally, they are very small indeed. Second, their distribution is far from uniform. If you live in the North, your chances of meeting anyone other than a fellow white Briton are clearly very small whilst, if you live in Greater London, it is markedly higher. As is widely known, the various ethnic minority groups have formed communities which, at the local level — that of a local government ward, for instance — may well approach 100 per cent, whilst others — by far the majority — remain exclusively white. This does much to explain their high visibility and the consequent misconceptions as to their national numbers. Table 1 clearly shows how, in spite of appearances, the minority groups, as a proportion of the total population, are correctly so called.

Most Caribbean settlers came over as complete families and needed appropriate housing for the wives and children from the beginning. They found these in local authority housing and they and their children have continued to do so. Karn (1983) makes a strong case for the argument that these high concentrations in selected estates were the result of actual, if not intentional, racist policies in

Table 1: Ethnic Group of Residents

Area	Total	Ethnic Group %								Other groups	
		White	Black Carib	Black Afr	Black other	Ind	Pak	Bang	Chi	Asian	Other
GREAT BRITAIN	54,888,844	94.5	0.9	0.4	0.3	1.5	0.9	0.3	0.3	0.4	0.5
England and Wales	49,890,277	94.1	1.0	0.4	0.4	1.7	0.9	0.3	0.3	0.4	0.5
England	47,055,204	93.8	1.1	0.4	0.4	1.8	1.0	0.3	0.3	0.4	0.5
Regions of England											
North	3,026,732	98.7	0.0	0.0	0.1	0.3	0.3	0.1	0.2	0.1	0.2
Tyne and Wear Met. Cty	1,095,152	98.2	0.0	0.1	0.1	0.4	0.3	0.3	0.3	0.1	0.2
Remainder	1,931,580	99.0	0.0	0.0	0.1	0.2	0.3	0.0	0.1	0.1	0.2
Yorks and Humberside	4,836,524	95.6	0.4	0.1	0.2	0.8	2.0	0.2	0.2	0.2	0.3
S Yorks Met. Cty.	1,262,630	97.1	0.5	0.1	0.2	0.3	1.0	0.1	0.2	0.1	0.4
W Yorks Met. Cty.	2,013,693	91.8	0.7	0.1	0.3	1.7	4.0	0.3	0.1	0.2	0.7
Remainder	1,560,201	99.0	0.0	0.1	0.1	0.2	0.1	0.1	0.1	0.1	0.2
East Midlands	3,953,372	95.2	0.6	0.1	0.3	2.5	0.4	0.1	0.2	0.2	0.4
East Anglia	2,027,004	97.9	0.2	0.1	0.4	0.3	0.3	0.1	0.2	0.2	0.3
South East	17,208,264	90.1	1.9	1.0	0.6	2.6	0.8	0.6	0.5	0.8	1.1
Greater London	6,679,699	79.8	4.4	2.4	1.2	5.2	1.3	1.3	0.8	1.7	1.9
Inner London	2,504,451	74.4	7.1	4.4	2.0	3.0	1.2	2.8	1.1	1.8	2.2
Outer London	4,175,248	83.1	2.7	1.3	0.7	6.5	1.4	0.4	0.7	1.6	1.6
Outer Met. Area	5,544,607	95.7	0.5	0.1	0.2	1.3	0.8	0.2	0.3	0.4	0.5
Outer South East	4,938,958	97.8	0.3	0.1	0.2	0.5	0.2	0.1	0.2	0.2	0.4
South West	4,609,424	98.6	0.3	0.1	0.1	0.2	0.1	0.1	0.1	0.1	0.3
West Midlands	5,150,187	91.8	1.5	0.1	0.4	3.1	1.9	0.4	0.2	0.2	0.4
W Mids. Met. Cty.	2,551,671	85.4	2.8	0.2	0.6	5.5	3.5	0.7	0.2	0.3	0.8
Remainder	2,598,516	98.0	0.2	0.0	0.1	0.7	0.4	0.1	0.1	0.1	0.3
North West	6,243,697	96.1	0.3	0.1	0.3	0.9	1.2	0.2	0.3	0.1	0.5
Greater Manchester M.C.	2,499,441	94.1	0.7	0.2	0.4	1.2	2.0	0.5	0.3	0.2	0.5
Merseyside Met. Cty.	1,403,642	98.2	0.2	0.2	0.3	0.2	0.1	0.1	0.4	0.1	0.2
Remainder	2,340,614	97.0	0.1	0.0	0.1	1.0	1.1	0.1	0.1	0.1	0.2
Wales	2,835,073	98.5	0.1	0.1	0.1	0.2	0.2	0.1	0.2	0.1	0.4
Scotland	4,998,567	98.7	0.0	0.1	0.1	0.2	0.4	0.0	0.2	0.1	0.2

Source: 1991 Census, OPCS.

public housing departments, reflecting the racism of society at large. Changes in the housing market since the 1960s have made it progressively more difficult for people on low incomes to become house-owners and with the reduction in numbers of houses at the disposal of local authorities, movement from one authority to another has become extremely difficult. Thus, the majority of Caribbean families find themselves trapped in local authority housing, their relative poverty making it impossible for them to buy their way out and housing department regulations constraining their movement within the system.

Migrants from India, with their different settlement strategy (where those from the Caribbean came over as whole families, Indian migrants arrived as single males) found it best to combine their resources and buy low-cost houses. Thus these houses were often all-male establishments, easily affordable out of their owners' combined incomes. With family reunification, savings plus a share of the equity made it possible for them to buy again. Present patterns are possibly the residual effect of a combination of available work and 'suitable' housing.

The Pakistani strategy was very similar to the Indian. There were two significant differences between them however. They started their migration later and began their family reunification later so that their opportunity to establish themselves was shorter before the economic climate changed for the worse.

The overall numbers of the Bangladeshi group are small by comparison with the other communities from South Asia. They are heavily concentrated in London and Greater Manchester. As the most recent arrivals, they had not had the time to build up an economic base as the Indians and, to a lesser extent, the Pakistanis had. The present economic climate in the region has resulted in the lamentable situation described later in this chapter. There seems little prospect of change for the better in the foreseeable future.

The East African Asian group is, as we attempt to show below, different from all others of South Asian origin. They were urbanized before arrival, essentially middle-class, they came as complete families and with financial resources. Their pattern of settlement reflects these facts and suggests that their ability to live and work where they choose is constrained by little more than that of their white peers.

Table 2 allows a comparison to be made between the numbers of white and ethnic minority people by gender and within selected age bands — 0–15, 16–29, 30–54 and over 54 years. It clearly shows that all ethnic minority groups have a greater proportion of young people in the younger age ranges (0–29) than is found in the same age range for the white population. There are some variations in this general pattern. Thus, the Caribbean community has a noticeable bulge in the 16–29 band which is not repeated in the youngest band, whilst the Chinese community remains virtually constant throughout. The most significant peaks in the age profiles occur in the South Asian communities — Indian, Pakistani and Bangladeshi — where the age bands 0–29 years show a marked rise in their proportion of the total population. Although the actual numbers in these groups are still small relative to the whites, their future increase in numbers is certain and as a proportion of the total population is probable.

Table 2: *Population of England: By Ethnic Origin and by Age*

Ages	Total Persons	White	Black Caribbean	Black African	Black Other	Indian	Pakistani	Bangladeshi	Chinese	Asian	Other
Total Persons	47,055,204	44,144,339	495,682	206,918	172,282	823,821	449,646	157,881	141,661	189,253	273,721
%	100	93.8	1.0	0.4	0.3	1.7	1.0	0.3	0.3	0.4	0.8
Total Males	22,812,889	21,358,956	237,217	103,685	84,390	414,220	231,785	82,228	69,705	89,600	141,103
%	100	93.6	1.0	0.5	0.4	1.8	1.0	0.4	0.3	0.4	0.6
Age 0–15	4,833,016	4,343,285	54,946	30,576	44,230	123,884	99,218	38,526	16,816	23,294	58,241
%	100	89.9	1.1	0.6	0.9	2.6	2.1	0.8	0.3	0.5	1.2
Age 16–29	4,861,921	4,498,741	62,814	31,598	24,673	95,306	52,597	18,035	21,389	22,806	33,962
%	100	92.5	1.3	0.6	0.5	2.0	1.1	0.4	0.4	0.5	0.7
Age 30–54	7,716,515	7,268,610	71,274	35,767	12,846	148,621	60,654	17,666	25,184	37,233	38,660
%	100	94.2	0.9	0.5	0.2	1.9	0.8	0.2	0.3	0.5	0.5
Age over 54	5,401,437	5,248,310	48,183	5,744	2,641	46,409	19,319	8,001	6,316	6,267	10,240
%	100	97.2	0.9	0.1	0.1	0.9	0.4	0.1	0.1	0.1	0.1
Total females	24,242,315	22,785,383	258,465	103,233	87,892	409,601	217,861	75,653	71,956	99,653	132,618
%	100	93.9	1.1	0.4	0.4	1.7	0.9	0.3	0.3	0.4	0.6
Age 0–15	4,603,286	4,132,421	53,622	30,468	43,210	119,582	93,525	36,138	15,855	22,726	56,043
%	100	89.8	1.2	0.7	0.9	2.6	2.0	0.8	0.3	0.5	1.2
Age 16–29	4,907,453	4,513,698	74,164	35,163	28,619	101,348	54,994	18,678	20,580	24,804	34,403
%	100	92.0	1.5	0.7	0.6	2.1	1.1	0.4	0.4	0.5	0.7
Age 30–54	7,760,302	7,293,158	90,511	34,352	13,494	146,856	57,245	18,059	28,917	45,338	32,392
%	100	94.0	1.2	0.4	0.2	1.9	0.7	0.2	0.4	0.6	0.4
Age over 54	6,971,249	6,835,104	40,168	3,553	2,569	41,815	12,097	2,778	6,603	6,785	9,776
%	100	98.0	0.6	0.1	<0.1	0.6	0.2	<0.1	0.1	0.1	0.1

Table 3: *Fertility Rates According to the Mother's Country of Birth*

Women born in	TPFR*
UK	1.8
Pakistan)	
)	4.9
Bangladesh)	
India	2.8
Africa	3.6
Caribbean	1.8
Far East (including China, Hong Kong, Malaysia and Singapore	1.9

Source: OPCS, 1990.
*TPFR: the Total Period Fertility Rate is the average number of children which would be born to a woman if she experienced the age-specific fertility rate current at the time throughout her childbearing span.

Much depends on the future family sizes in these communities. Table 3 gives the total period fertility rates for significant ethnic minority groups. This makes it clear that the completed family sizes for the minority groups from South Asia (particularly those from Bangladesh and Pakistan) are very significantly greater than for white families in the UK. How long this will continue to be true is uncertain. The Office of Populations Census and Surveys (OPCS) has generally assumed that fertility rates of ethnic minority women will, in time, fall to the general level of the UK. In the absence of any real evidence one way or another, we can only express our opinion, which is that the rate at which reductions in fertility may take place are likely to vary substantially from one ethnic group to another and that some, if they fall at all in the foreseeable future, will fall very slowly indeed.

The Minority Communities

The South Asian communities in Britain (Indians, Pakistanis and Bangladeshis) now number well over a million people. They share certain characteristics — most of the first generation settlers are still inspired by their upbringing in the Indian sub-Continent which remains more significant in their everyday lives than their more recent British experience. Their skin colour also identifies their origins and makes them ready targets for racial prejudice. It would be wrong, however, to regard them as being members of a single community.

The Bangladeshi Community

To understand the general nature of the Bangladeshi settlers in Britain it is necessary to say something of the history of Bangladesh itself and the process by which many, perhaps most of those settlers came in large numbers from quite small areas of the country as a whole.

Bangladesh came into being in 1971 before which it was known as East Pakistan which had itself been created in 1947 following the partition of India. Before that, the area was known as East Bengal. The concept underlying the formation of Pakistan was essentially religious: it was to be a Muslim state where its people could conduct their affairs, free from the influence of the Hindus who, it was alleged, since the fall of the Mughal Empire, had dominated them and others with different religious beliefs.

For present-day Bangladesh, religion is both a cohesive and divisive force. It is certainly one of the most powerful forces contributing to the maintenance of its society. Muslims make up 85 per cent of its population with the remainder including Hindus, Buddhists and Christians.

Islam is mono-theistic and teaches equality to its believers. Its principles were revealed by Allah to his prophet Mohammed and are preserved in the Koran. It advocates a brotherhood of man under Allah and knows no barriers of race or nation. Thus a Muslim family in Bangladesh will resemble more closely another Muslim family in Nigeria (or Oldham) than a Hindu family in Bangladesh.

There are five religious duties incumbent on all Muslims:

- the acceptance of one God, Allah, and his prophet Mohammed,
- the profession of faith,
- the giving of alms,
- fasting during the month of Ramadan,
- pilgrimage to Mecca.

There is no separation of spiritual and temporal or religious and secular activities in Islam. For a Muslim, religion, law and social organization are combined, so that injunctions extend beyond religious practices to aspects of conduct which, in Western society, are regulated (if at all) by secular law and civil authority.

Unlike Hindu society, the structure of Muslim society is not based on caste. However, during the Mughal Empire concepts of class emerged with an *Ashraf* or upper class (often with claims to be of Persian descent) and an *Atraf* or lower class — essentially the rulers and the ruled. With the arrival of the British in India these divisions were maintained even though their basis was unclear and not well understood. The Permanent Settlement Act of 1793 established permanently settled estates with the revenue from the land being paid to Zamindars who thus became tax-farmers. They identified themselves with the Ashraf class and as land-holders were certainly in a better position than the landless peasantry. By the 1950s this group had largely lost its connexion with the land and had become influential in government, politics and commerce. Social mobility was highly constrained but not impossible. Some peasants' sons were able, through scholarships or the efforts of their fathers, to reach the highest levels of education. This in turn opened up opportunities to develop careers in commerce and the government service and become eligible to marry into upper-class families who were quite prepared to 'co-opt' them in recognition of their character and achievements.

In the 1830s the tea growing industry was established in Assam (then part of East Bengal) and workers were imported from other parts of India such as Bihar and Orissa, to work the plantations in preference to the local people. Alam (1988) argues convincingly that the locals, largely from the district of Sylhet, were used to carry the tea down to Calcutta where their contracts were terminated. They then looked for jobs in the port area of Hoogly and some of them got jobs on ships. Some of them may have then become professional seafarers but for the majority, who would be given the meanest and worst-paid jobs on board, the ship was just a means of seeking their fortunes elsewhere and they were likely to jump ship at the first opportunity. Of these, some found themselves in England where they settled.

However, they retained contact with their homeland and relations through letters in which they described their new country and their successes in it. It was these pioneers and their descendants who set in motion the process of chain migration which remained at very modest levels until the early 1960s when Pakistan was requested by Britain to supply manpower for industries which were unable to attract sufficient numbers of white indigenous workers. Although the numbers of early (pre-1960) migrants were modest, they do account for the surprisingly high proportion of settlers from Sylhet in Britain generally and the North-West in particular. It hardly needs emphasizing that the motives of these immigrants were essentially economic. They were, in general, amongst the most impoverished of Sylhet who came to Britain in an attempt to make their fortunes.

There is little doubt that for the majority of these Bangladeshis the intention was to make money which would enable them to return to their homeland and purchase property and businesses. Of the sample interviewed by Alam, 90 per cent remitted money home to their families on a regular basis and in other respects retained close ties with their homeland. This took the form of regular and quite often extended visits to Bangladesh for what were usually described as 'business' or 'family' reasons and often consisted of family marriages, property issues and the like. For this group of settlers, the myth of return — that is, the belief that having made their fortunes in Britain, they and their children would return to Bangladesh to enjoy the fruits of their long exile — was, and remains, very powerful.

In addition to these economic migrants, there were considerable numbers of well-educated, relatively wealthy, urban young Bangladeshis who had been students at the country's most prestigious university in Dacca. They came to Britain to get the higher qualifications at British universities, with a view to returning, groomed for one of the top jobs in Bangladesh. Many did return but many stayed behind or returned to Britain after a brief and unsatisfying experience of their homeland. For this group, their primary socialization as the children of wealthy Bangladeshis, followed by the formation of powerful personal networks at the

University of Dacca and in British universities, meant that they have remained in close touch with each other.

Finally, there was a third group, also graduates, but of provincial colleges and universities in Bangladesh, whose qualifications were held in lower esteem than those awarded by the University of Dacca. The relatively low esteem in which their degrees were held made it sensible for them to come to Britain with the intention of getting professional qualifications in banking or accountancy, for example, before returning home. Few, according to Alam, realized this ambition and found it difficult to return as 'failures'. It should be emphasized that of those Bangladeshis now settled in Britain, those falling into the last two categories form a small proportion of the total.

For the best-educated and wealthy in the 1950s, most in fact returned to East Pakistan (now Bangladesh) where their job opportunities and prospects of a career were very good. During the 1960s these opportunities decreased and many more decided to remain in Britain or returned, disillusioned, after a short period at home. The situation was complicated for both groups of the educated classes by the turmoil surrounding the birth of Bangladesh. Political considerations became important and whilst many of the right-wing students returned, left-wing students found it prudent to remain in Britain. The same period saw large numbers of well-educated, wealthy families migrating to Britain as well as to other European countries, the USA and Canada where as doctors, engineers or the like, they found no difficulty in retaining their economic and social status.

For the majority of the Bangladeshi population in the North-West — those from Sylhet who came in search of work, largely in the cotton industry — a recent survey of 580 households provides disquieting reading (Oldham Metropolitan Borough Council, 1990). We do not suggest that its findings are precisely generalizable for all areas of Bangladeshi settlement in Britain but we do believe that, in broad brush terms, similar surveys would provide comparable results.

It shows a very young population: 57 per cent of the 3,857 were under the age of 15 (as compared with 20.4 per cent for the total population living within the authority's boundaries). This goes some way towards explaining the family sizes: 26.7 per cent were living in households of eight or more persons. This may be compared with 0.13 per cent of the local white population. Only 15.5 per cent of Bangladeshis were living in households of three or four persons: for the local white population this accounted for almost 33.5 per cent. Most (68 per cent) of the houses were owner occupied, 13 per cent were rented from the council, 10 per cent were privately rented and the remainder were owned by housing associations or others. Using the Bedroom Standard to assess the level of occupancy, almost 71 per cent live in overcrowded conditions with the worst conditions being found in owner-occupied houses. The General Household Survey suggests that, nationally, 4 per cent of households live in overcrowded conditions and 65 per cent under-occupy their houses.

In terms of employment for the Bangladeshi males aged 16+, 35 per cent were in full-time work, 1.7 per cent in part-time work, 13 per cent were full-time students, 38 per cent were unemployed and the remainder were permanently sick, disabled or wholly retired. For females, 2.8 per cent were in full-time work, 2.2 per cent were in part-time work, 6.5 per cent were full-time students, 4.5 per cent were unemployed, 81.7 per cent were engaged in housework and the remainder were permanently sick, disabled or wholly retired. Of males in employment, only 6.0 per cent were categorized as professional, managerial and non-manual, 5.7 per cent were skilled manual, 81.6 per cent were semi-skilled manual and the remainder unskilled or inadequately described. Comparable figures for the general male population are 14 per cent semi-skilled manual and 43 per cent as non-manual. Local authority calculations showed that for the Bangladeshi community, the dependency rate (the number of non-active persons — i.e. the total population minus the labour force — expressed as a ratio of those active) is 6.91 non-active persons for every active person i.e. 6.91:1. The equivalent rate for the North-West as a whole is 1.1:1. We should add that, alarming though these figures are, they do not take into account the virtual certainty that, in addition to the dependants living with them, some of the income made by those in work will be remitted to parents and other more or less dependant relatives living in Bangladesh.

A lower proportion of the members of this Bangladeshi community were in various forms of tertiary education than their white peers. Of those aged between 16–49 years, 2.75 per cent of males and 5.66 per cent of females were studying at polytechnics or universities as compared to national figures of 32.0 per cent for males and 21.0 per cent for females. Of Bangladeshi males and females, 39.45 per cent and 18.87 per cent respectively, were registered with some form of Further Education College as compared to national figures of 44 per cent and 51 per cent.

Language skills were assessed by the head of household for each member of the family. On that basis 82 per cent of males and 42 per cent of females aged between 16–29 were able to speak English either fluently or fairly well and similar figures were returned for reading in English — 83 per cent and 42 per cent respectively. Gender variations were even more apparent for the older (30–44) members where the ability to speak English fluently or fairly well fell to 50.6 per cent for males and 3.9 per cent for females. The figures for those able to read English either fluently or fairly well were 41.1 per cent for males and 2.9 per cent for females.

The report from which these statistics have been extracted concludes with the following statement:

> The level of social and economic deprivation which this community faces would lead one to be very concerned about the continuing cycle of deprivation which will be very hard to break. The indications are that such a cycle of deprivation would mean that there would be a continued need for special support from a number of Council departments. (Oldham Metropolitan Borough Council, 1990)

The history of Bangladesh and its people who came to settle in Britain briefly sketched out above ensured that virtually all follow Islam. Social class appears to have a major impact on the effect that their belief has on their daily lives as presented in public. Many of the best-educated, effectively middle-class members of the community, have adopted social and interpersonal styles which have enabled them to retain their religious beliefs as a keystone of their cultural heritage in their private lives whilst adapting to many of the social and other demands of living in Britain. The effect of this adaptation is particularly evident in the degree of freedom which males are prepared to allow, and sometimes encourage, in the lives of their female relatives and the ways in which these women are able to claim and exercise that freedom.

However, for the great majority of settlers, cultural, religious, economic and linguistic factors combine to make adaptation to British society difficult. The first generation of settlers, who form the majority of the group, brought with them a strong religious belief which has probably intensified under the effects of racial intolerance and what is perceived as religious hostility most clearly evidenced by the publication of *The Satanic Verses* and the events arising from it. As Parekh (1989) observed at the time:

> ...we should not see ethnicity as something fixed and unchanging. Historically speaking, every community has felt forced to accept change, to at least come to terms with other communities. The question is, when do communities become frozen? When do they say they will not change any more? I think that happens when they feel besieged, threatened, when no space is left for them to grow.

It is our impression that the Bangladeshi community is currently in that situation. Its senior members feel trapped in an alien society and are best able to make sense of their lives by looking to their religious and cultural roots in Bangladesh which they seek to impose on their families. Many continue to believe that their original intention — to make their fortunes and return with their families to Bangladesh — may yet be accomplished. It is this vision which does much to account for the strategies that they have adopted to deal with the pressures of British society.

It should also be noted that Islam is different from, for example, Christianity in its relative inflexibility. Whereas the Bible is perceived by most Christians as a record of the progressive revelation of God's nature and his will towards mankind, the Koran is deemed to be Allah's complete and perfect revelation of himself to Mohammed. Thus Christianity has had from its inception a tradition of re-evaluation and change in changing circumstances. Islam has no such tradition. On the contrary, the truths of the Koran are seen as immutable. For those whose personal identities are formulated in Koranic terms, the achievement of room to manoeuvre requires a high degree of religious and personal sophistication. For many of the Bangladeshi community, this sort of sophistication is not sought for nor is its pursuit encouraged by many religious leaders.

Among the more obvious effects of the practice of Islam are those relating to the position of women within the family and in society. Although the Koran gives women the rights to equal education, to earn and possess money and to inherit, control and dispose of property without the consent of husbands and fathers (rights withheld from British women until the Married Women's Property Act in the latter part of the nineteenth century), their position in society as seen by Western eyes is not enviable. Purdah (the seclusion of women) is widely practised, though this varies from one community to another and is much affected by levels of education and by social class. The free mixing of the sexes is strongly discouraged, thus it is difficult for women to take paid employment outside the home. Modesty of dress at all times is required.

That is not to say, however, that for individuals, and particularly young people within the Bangladeshi community, movement towards partial acculturation is not happening. Weinreich and Kelly (1990) reporting on a study made of 20 male and 20 female Muslims aged about 17 years show how attitudes towards issues such as authority within the family, the choice of marriage partner, the level of desirable personal freedom, the importance that should be attached to the opinions of others and the like, show marked variations between males and females. Among other conclusions they observe:

> The 'progressive' young Muslim women have identified with individualist values to the extent that they wish for greater individual choice and less community surveillance of their behaviour. However, their redefinition of their ethnic identity remains quite distinct from the female version of Anglo-Saxon identity with its strongly individualist orientation . . . While demonstrating their integration into the wider Anglo-Saxon milieu, their identities have not become assimilated within it. They retain their distinctiveness intact . . .

> . . . the 'progressive' young women [have] the most to win within the Anglo-Saxon context; but the 'orthodox' young women [are] the most unbending according to context, in which they retain their high self-evaluation within the Anglo-Saxon context by virtue of maintaining intact their orientation towards orthodoxy.

The Bangladeshi community is essentially 'collectivist'. That is to say its members perceive themselves not only as individuals but also as members of a group — the family. Nor does it end there; the family honour requires that the family and its members enjoy the respect of the wider community. This can perhaps be best understood by comparing their perceptions with the emphasis placed by Western European cultures on personal goals and initiatives with their concomitant high regard for independence. As Weinreich and Kelly (1990) observe, these notions of personal conscience and responsibility are particularly powerful in those parts of Western Europe that have been exposed to the Protestant Christian faith. In such societies, interpersonal relations (and even relationships between members of the same family) are deemed to be a matter for negotiation between the individuals concerned. Although individuals remain dependent in varying degrees on others, government and the law, as well as others in their society, regard them as responsible for their own affairs. Such notions contrast sharply with the collectivist society in which there is a much greater emphasis on the responsibility of the individual to the extended family which, in turn, is monitored and regulated by the wider community.

The Pakistani Community

The Pakistani communities in Britain were drawn by the possibility of work in British industry during the boom following World War II. Many of them came from Mirpur in Pakistani-held Kashmir. Other pressures leading to their migration were the political turmoil associated with partition and the dispute over Kashmir, loss of land arising from extensive dam construction and an affiliation to Britain resulting from a long tradition of service in the British army. Their objectives were very similar to those of the Punjabis. The initial aim of the Mirpuris was to acquire capital and return to Pakistan. However, their corporate experiences have been markedly different.

This is partly explicable by the relative poverty of their homeland and the low level of skills that they brought with them but an array of other factors, social, religious and cultural, have ensured that their past experience, their present position and their future prospects in British society will differ from their Indian peers. Like them, the Pakistani immigrants took on unskilled or semi-skilled work in Britain (mainly in the Midlands and the North in heavy engineering or the textiles industries) but unlike them, they were still in their original occupations when the industries in which they were working collapsed in the early 1980s. By comparison with the Indian settlers — either Sikh or Hindu — they have remained in highly concentrated communities, largely in inner-city areas, the process of family reunification was started much later and they have been economically less successful.

In order to begin to understand the Pakistani communities in Britain, it is necessary to look at the nature of their society in Pakistan. Ballard (1990) strongly emphasizes the relative poverty of Mirpur but argues that other domestic, cultural and religious factors must be taken into account. The Maharaja of Kashmir had milked the peasantry for all they were worth and provided little in return (in 1947 there were no metalled roads and only two high schools in the entire district) and in the war with India which followed partition, the local bourgeoisie fled to India. Since then, it would be fair to say, India has been more successful in setting and achieving economic goals than Pakistan.

Pakistani marriage customs differ from Sikh and Hindu practice in that they encourage endogamy and marriage between cousins is common. The bride is thus a member of the family almost as much before as after her marriage and the *biraderi* (brotherhood — a complex of relationships both of blood and by marriage) is powerfully strengthened by its members being often related by a network of liaisons. Also, because the bride does not bring her own external network of family relationships, the marriage intensifies the unity of the extended family and makes it the more difficult for younger couples (with or without their children) to form autonomous units — even covertly — within the extended household. Ballard (1990) records that his observations in Mirpur suggest that well over half the marriages are between first cousins. This leads to a much more inward-looking family and, he argues convincingly, such relationships have had a major impact on the process of migration to Britain.

The pioneer settlers were, by definition, without existing contacts in Britain. Thereafter the build-up of Pakistani migrants was powerfully affected by the magnetic attraction of existing members of the family. 'Thus', Ballard writes, 'despite their location thousands of miles from home, most migrants continued to live and work alongside their kinsmen and fellow villagers.' Their intention, to earn money not for their own benefit but so that they could send much of what they were able to save to their family in Pakistan, was clear and consistent. The personal costs were very high in terms of loss of contact with their wives and children. They became great travellers, flying home to renew contact on a regular basis. Why, it might be asked, did they not follow the example of the Sikhs and Hindus and start to bring their families over to Britain? There were a number of reasons.

First, and most obviously to Western eyes, it reduced their ability to save. Four or five could not live as cheaply as one, and the object of their time spent working in Britain was to increase the wealth of the extended family, the *biraderi*, not the economic advancement of one unit within it. Second, in common with other South Asian men, whilst they might be impressed with the material advantages of working in Britain, they perceived much in its society as morally corrupt — and as Muslims, nowhere more so than in the behaviour of Western women. The Muslim rules of *purdah*, followed with particular rigour in Mirpur, require that adult women should avoid being seen in all public places, so that even shopping, for example, is done by the men of the family. The effect that purdah has on the mobility of women hardly needs stressing: what is perhaps worth noting is the converse effect — the additional force it gives to an already strong tendency for the family to be an enclosed, relatively immobile, inward-looking unit. Third, the complex network of relationships that made up the family, arising from their marriage customs outlined above, by which the man's wife was almost certainly related to other women of the family in Mirpur before, as well as after marriage, made her migration to Britain much more of a wrench than would be the case for Hindu and Sikh women. Fourth, the fact of setting up house in Britain signalized an autonomy of one unit of the family that was contrary to all normal cultural expectations. Fifth, whilst the intention to return might be as powerful as ever, the reunification between husbands and their wives and children was a tacit admission that the return was to be long-delayed.

Against these forces acting on the men to persist in their single state in Britain and travel in order to see their families and maintain their social and emotional ties with Mirpur were others that ultimately became more compelling. There were, of course, the emotional hardships that were inescapable and could only be slightly diminished by the tide of letters, telephone calls and recorded messages that flooded backwards and forwards between Britain and Pakistan. However, if they had been at all, it seems possible that the decision to bring over their families would have been even further delayed. The deciding factor was the increasingly stringent legislation governing immigration and the less publicized but even more oppressive regulations and procedures adopted by the immigration service to enforce it.

This brief outline of some of the religious, social and cultural factors active in forming Pakistani society leads us to an attempt to characterize the British communities. First, all those customs and practices which created the 'inwardness' in the family in Pakistan are equally powerful here in Britain. The *biraderi* system of kinship still operates. Many women have been required to conform to an increasingly traditional regime as the men react with growing anxiety and suspicion to a British society which they perceive as being racist, permissive and secular. As a result of this, allied to a sense of isolation and hostility and international trends in the Muslim world, they are subjected to a stricter form of purdah.

Moreover, the marriage of close relatives, drawn either from the homeland or, increasingly, from those who have grown up in Britain, is re-creating those social conditions which militate against geographical mobility so that the Pakistani communities remain in dense concentrations. Whilst this undoubtedly gives a sense of security as well as satisfying other social and emotional needs, it significantly reduces the opportunities of members of the communities to acquire the kinds of skills necessary for economic and social success in the British context.

Nor does it seem probable that these skills will be acquired by many of the children now coming through the British education system. There seem to be regional variations in the benefits they gain. In some areas (Bradford for example) they are growing up in districts which are predominantly — often exclusively — Pakistani. Their mothers have never had the opportunity to learn English and the children's first language is their parents' mother tongue. The majority of their peers at school are like them so that English is only used in formal communications with their teachers. It is hardly surprising therefore that many do not achieve a very high level of proficiency and underachieve across the curriculum. After leaving school, they are re-immersed in the community and such English skills as they had are under-used and become even more inadequate. Elsewhere, it is apparent that parental aspirations for their children are high and they have adopted positive attitudes towards school and work. Their young people take more examinations, stay at school longer and go to college more often than their English peers. They have an intrinsic motivation towards achievement, blaming themselves rather than external factors such as discrimination for failure to achieve their goals (Verma, 1986). Since failure to achieve goals because of extrinsic rather than intrinsic factors is frequent, the social identity of Pakistani young people is probably in a state of transition as the alienation imposed by racial discrimination becomes increasingly apparent to them.

Young people born in Britain have had to acquire a typical dual identity as they were exposed to British mass media, education and socialization. Though remaining loyal to Islamic culture, incipient or actual conflicts between parents and children over such issues as dress, friends and activities outside the home have frequently developed. Parents have become increasingly concerned to ensure the effective transmission of religion and culture to their children. The example of the success of the Jewish community in protecting their religion and culture is often cited by Pakistanis as an example to be emulated.

The networks of mutual help and information *within* the communities are highly effective. The fact that many members in any given community are likely to come from the same or neighbouring villages and are probably related to each other ensures that this is so. However, these factors, allied to the alienation from British society at large, also ensure that there is still massive ignorance about much of British society that its indigenous members take for granted and which other South Asian communities — the East African Asians, Sikhs and Hindus — have much greater access to.

Migration and adaptation have been stressful experiences for many Pakistanis.

The advantages of sociability and collective life are balanced by the intensity of disputes when they arise, the pressure to conform, the harsh treatment of deviants and the potentially malicious role of gossip. (Khan, 1979)

The Indian Community

Hugh Tinker (1977) has characterized the 'overseas emigrants from India, Pakistan and Bangladesh' as part of the Banyan Tree whose roots travel far underground to form new trees, but always connected with the main growth. By this analogy, the South Asian immigrants retain strong emotional and cultural ties with the motherland, even several generations after migration.

The image of the Banyan tree to describe the spread of Indian civilization is taken from the writings of Tagore. It is, as Tinker points out, an idealistic one and another image is possible which presents the Indian emigrants as adaptable and opportunistic people, fitting themselves intelligently into new cultures, not stressing in overt ways a particular religious or cultural pattern which might be offensive to a host society. This is the model of the sapling, not the Banyan tree. Both models have some virtue and to understand this paradox it is necessary to turn to the history of the Hindu people in the Indian sub-continent.

The history, size and terrain of India ensure that no brief section such as this can do justice to the variety of its peoples who have come to settle in Britain. It is only possible to provide thumbnail sketches of two of the major religious groups, which may give the reader's powers of empathy some materials to work on.

Indian Hindus

As noted in the introduction to the Bangladeshi community, present-day India is the product of the partition which established the independence of both India and Pakistan. The intention was to enable Pakistan to come into being as an independent Muslim state and most (though not all) Muslims moved from what is now India into Pakistan. Of those that remained, the great majority were Hindus though Muslims remained the second largest religious group. There were also Buddhists, Sikhs, Jains, Parsees and Jews. The major distinction between India and Pakistan is that, whereas the latter is Muslim, India is a multi-religious country and the Constitution of the country has designated it a secular State. However, as recent events in India make clear, the secularization of the State does not mean that Hinduism is unimportant at the individual level or that it cannot form the basis of powerful political movements.

There are eighteen main languages in India with quite different scripts, and these may be subdivided into over 100 dialects which differ substantially from each other. The national language is Hindi but an Indian will speak the language of his own district first and Hindi as his second language. The ability to speak, read and write English remains a prerequisite for those who have ambitions in education and the government service. Thus a person born in the Gujerat will speak Gujerati as a first language, Hindi as a second and may well speak English as a third before leaving school.

The word 'Hindu' originated from the Persian and originally referred to a person who lived near the river Indus and who had not become a Muslim (Wheeler, 1966; 1968). The use of the word in connexion with religion probably came with the Muslim invasions of India when the Arabic name for India was Hindustan which means land of the Hindu people (Verma and Mallick, 1981). Unlike most religions, Hinduism has no prophet or founder but has rather grown and developed over some thousands of years, taking in new ideas from the various peoples who inhabited the country. Basham (1959) defined a Hindu as 'a man who chiefly bases his beliefs and way of life on the complex system of faiths and practices which has grown up organically in the Indian sub-continent over a period of at least three millennia.'

What makes Hinduism so difficult to describe is not only its vague nature but its variety and flexibility. It has no creed and its adherents can and do vary in their beliefs and practices. To a non-Hindu, it presents itself as a baffling tangle of myths with endless numbers of gods and goddesses. Behind all this variety, however, there lies a belief in one Supreme Divine Being. Among all this apparent fluidity, there are elements, such as the caste system, which are extraordinarily rigid. Nehru (1961) in an attempt to summarize it came to the conclusion that 'Its essential spirit seems to be to live and let live.'

Hindu scriptures have been collected over many years. Some of the earliest are collections of hymns and songs to gods and goddesses. These, with the commentaries on them (*Brahmanas*) and discussions of their meanings (*Upanishads*) are called *Vedas* (knowledge). The most popular of these is the *Bhagavad Gita* (Song of the Lord) which deeply influenced Mahatma Gandhi.

The gods take many different forms including those of many animals and the fire elements. However, most Hindus would say that there is only one God (Brahman) who may be worshipped in many different forms or incarnations (*avatars*) both male and female. Hindus believe that people live a series of lives. The soul passes through many bodies and different forms, each incarnation being a reward or punishment based on the virtues shown in the previous life.

An extraordinary feature of Hinduism is its durability. For 700 years until independence in 1947, major parts of India were ruled by non-Hindus (and often non-Indians) but this seems to have had little or no influence on the belief of its peoples. As Radhakrishnan (1971) wrote, 'The Hindu culture seems to possess some vitality which seems to be denied to other, more forceful currents. It is no more necessary to dissect Hinduism than to open a tree to see whether the sap still runs.'

A central feature of Hindu societies is that it has for centuries been built on a rigid system of castes. A caste is a group of people with a particular place in society and as Hinnels and Sharpe (1972) write:

A Hindu is a Hindu not because he accepts certain doctrines or philosophies but because he is a member of a caste. Hence it is, strictly speaking, impossible to become a Hindu, other than by being born into a caste.

The caste into which a Hindu was born and which established the duties which were expected of him was determined by the totality of his actions in his previous life. Originally there were four castes: *Brahmins*, literally 'priests' though in practice they did not necessarily perform the functions of priests as normally understood; *Kshatrias*, the rulers and warriors; *Vaisyas*, merchants and artisans; and *Sudras*, servants whose duty it was to serve the members of other castes. Outside the caste system altogether there has existed from ancient times a group who were known as the 'untouchables' who performed tasks such as slaughtering, cleaning latrines and other work which was thought to be degrading. They were not allowed to enter the temples or participate fully in religious ceremonies. These were called the *Harijans* (children of God) by Mahatma Gandhi who campaigned against the system.

Over a long period of time, these original four have been developed into a highly complicated structure of castes and sub-castes, each with its own customs, duties, traditions, morals and codes. Caste is both the doing and undoing of Hindu civilization. A specialized warrior caste was quite inadequate to defend the country against successive waves of attack from Persia and Hindu civilization suffered much wretchedness and confusion as a result. The colonial enterprises of the British, Dutch and Portuguese were able to exploit the internal divisions of Hindu society to their own advantage. The most decisive cause of Hindu defeats was Hindu disunity. Yet, despite continual subjugation and disorganization, Hindu society and religious culture has survived remarkably intact.

The caste system has been officially abolished by the Indian government and many Harijans are to be found at all levels of government. However, though the position of the State on this issue is clear and enshrined in its Constitution, the actual attitudes of many of the people are at least ambivalent, as witnessed by the fall of V.P. Singh's government in November 1990. Although there were a number of issues which made it inevitable, the one ultimately seized upon to unite opposition to him was that of compensatory (positive) action in favour of 'depressed classes' — substantially the Harijans.

Marriage partners are normally found by parents for their children from within their own caste if they are Brahmins. For members of other castes this is still usual but not invariable.

Most Indians in Britain are from the Punjab and Gujerat and are Hindus. Whilst there are numerous temples and shrines in India, there is only a handful in Britain. Many families often join together and hire a hall on Sundays where services are held, but it is from the daily observances in the home that Hinduism gains its strength.

Emigration from the Indian sub-continent is not, by and large, seen by its practitioners as a method of escape from poverty; rather it is a mode of advancement for certain aspirant groups who already have a particular social identity. For them, emigration is a viable option when a suitable opportunity arises. Structural opportunities and changes — war, partition, famine, land-loss, have been the stimuli for many, but not the ultimate cause.

The Punjabi Sikh Community

Ballard (1989) estimates that at least two-thirds and possibly as many as three-quarters of all British South Asians are of Indians of Punjabi origin. Of these Punjabis, the majority, though by no means all, are Sikhs of the Jat (peasant farmer) caste from the Jullundur district. The earliest pioneers found their way to Britain between the wars as itinerant pedlars and during the post-war boom acted as the magnets which drew their kinsmen and started the process of chain migration.

The word 'Sikh' derives from an ancient word meaning discipline. Sikhism started as a result of the teaching of Guru Nanak (Guru means religious teacher) who was born in Lahore (now in Pakistan) some 500 years ago. He encouraged all people to worship God truthfully. He believed that there was one God and that all people could reach him. There followed a succession of ten Gurus of whom the tenth, Guru Govind Singh, introduced the concept of *khalsa* or brotherhood into which all Sikhs are baptized.

From about the age of eleven years, a Sikh may go through a form of baptism into the *khalsa* thus becoming a soldier saint and embracing the five Ks which are the outward signs of Sikhism. These are *kesh* (uncut hair, closely identified with the wearing of a turban); *kanga* (comb); *kirpan* (short dagger); *kara* (steel bracelet) and *kach* (an undergarment). Sikhism rejected the caste system and all males take the name Singh (lion) and all females the name Kaur (princess). Baptized Sikhs also agree to abstain from alcohol, tobacco, ritually slaughtered foods and immorality.

Sikhs meet to worship in a *Gurdwara* (temple) and, before entering, they remove their shoes and cover their heads. The Gurdwara is frequently a multi-purpose building with parts of it acting as a community centre for local Sikhs.

As with most of the other migrants, the intention of the early arrivals was to earn and save as much money as possible before returning home. This having been said, poverty was not, in many cases, their primary or most pressing motive. Many had served in the British army during World War II and the experience of partition made migration to Britain seem an attractive proposition. However, most found it necessary to stay longer than they first intended and for many, the rapid decay of the textiles and allied industries in Britain made even delayed return difficult. For a variety of reasons, including changes in the immigration laws (see Ballard, 1989 for a more detailed account), by the mid-1960s it became the norm for wives and families to join their husbands relatively quickly after their arrival. Newcomers would work for two or three years to pay off any debts and buy a house when they would be joined by their families. This early reunification resulted in a very rapid development of normal social life within the Sikh communities and the re-creation of family and kinship networks which helped to provide mutual support systems — both social and financial.

We would stress the importance of this in the rapid development of the Sikh community by briefly outlining the general principles involved. In the Punjab a family unit is conceived of as a man, his sons, their sons, wives and unmarried daughters who all live together under the same roof and work to the common good. Marriage to members of the family on either the father's or mother's side is prohibited but is normally to a member of the same caste. In practice this means that wives have to be sought from another village. After marriage, the bridegroom's primary loyalty remains to his extended family though the bride brings her own network of kinsfolk who may form a valuable set of allies and support. Once the marriage was well-established and had produced children, it was common for it to achieve some measure of autonomy, even though this was not encouraged. Thus, whilst there were strong pressures which militated against the men sending for their wives and setting up house in Britain there were countervailing customs which made it acceptable for them to do so. Once the decision was made, the Sikh community was able to re-create a viable society in Britain, and was one of the earliest of the South Asian groups to do so.

They were thus in as good a position as any of the minority groups to face the problems brought about by the recession of the late 1970s and early 1980s and the collapse of the manufacturing industries in which many of them had worked since their arrival. Though even here, the results of the recession were felt more acutely by some than others. Those living in the south-east were affected less than those living in the industrial north and those with high level skills that were transferable from one occupation to another were less affected than those who were only semi-skilled or whose skills were not readily transferable.

What appears to have happened is that many of those made redundant have sought to become self-employed. As a strategy it made sense because their chances of paid employment in a contracting British industry, in competition with white applicants who were also the victims of redundancy, were poor indeed. The Labour Force Survey of 1986 shows that 20 per cent of all male Indians (not all of whom are Sikhs of course) were self-employed. In electing for this strategy, it was inevitable that, for many, the enterprise had to be one that required little in the way of initial capital but which could be built up by hard work (Ballard, 1989). The attraction of market stalls, small shops, restaurants, and motor repairs is then readily understood. Those selling clothes in markets soon perceived that, given the traditional domestic skills of wives and female relatives, it would be easy to make them at home as well as sell them, and at greater profit. The most successful have done very well and now employ large numbers of women working at home — often Punjabi Muslims whose culture and customs prevent them from taking paid employment outside the home, though the extremely low wages that many receive for their work is crucial to the financial survival of the family.

Their success has been signalized by movement away from the low-cost housing originally acquired to better locations in the suburbs (and beyond) and the adoption of what is recognizably a middle-class lifestyle. The children of this generation, born and educated in Britain, have done well at school and afterwards at colleges and universities (Tomlinson, 1990) but still face the problems of finding employment commensurate with their qualifications. Those with qualifications that are not in shortage areas and are not readily exploitable outside an institutional context are turning to business enterprises of one kind and another and whilst they may feel, with reason, that their career intentions have been unjustly frustrated, will probably do well.

This is not least the result of a combination of characteristics of Sikh families and societies identified by many students (Macleod, 1976; Pettigrew, 1972; Ballard, 1989; Bachu 1985, among others). These may be summarized as follows. Within the family, brothers and other descendants of the male line are at once highly supportive of, and in competition with, each other. 'They are', as Ballard puts it, 'simultaneously allies and rivals.' Between families there is strong competition for success. This is partly the result of the teachings of the Gurus who advocated an egalitarian society which encourages the belief that Jack is as good as his master and partly their abolition of a hierarchical caste system such as is found in Hindu societies which stratifies their society and makes upward migration extraordinarily difficult. 'Thus, if an individual works hard and makes money and skilfully creates a set of links, he can become a person of importance. Achieved status is what is important' (Pettigrew, 1972). This is a potent recipe for upward mobility and economic success. Whilst the religious, cultural and personal forces acting on the Sikhs in Britain may not be well understood by many of the white community, their outward behaviour and responses to the challenge of making their way in it are notably congruent with that adopted by the more successful of their white peers.

The East African Asians

Whilst the members of other South Asian groups are, with a few individual exceptions, direct migrants, the East African Asians are, by definition, a group apart. They did not come direct from the Indian sub-continent, they arrived by way of Kenya, Uganda and Tanzania. The consequences of this to the nature of the group and the identity of its members can scarcely be over-estimated. As Brooks and Singh (1978–9) observe:

> we accept obviously that East African Asians come from a number of ethnic groups. Nevertheless, it is apparent to us that the East African experience is so important that it cuts across ethnic divisions and, for the purpose of our argument, it is appropriate to group East African Asians together . . .

The Labour Force Survey of 1983 suggested that there were some 163,000 East African Asians resident in Britain, of whom 159,000 were of Indian and 4,000 of Pakistani origin. The major cause of their first migration — to Africa — was the construction of the Kenya-Uganda railway. They were mainly Sikhs of the Ramgarhia (artisan) caste, though they also included some Hindus and Muslims, and they remained in Africa for some sixty years during which time many of them rose to occupy essentially middle-class positions in society. Ghai (1965) suggests that 36 per cent of Asians were in executive, administrative and managerial positions, about 25 per cent were skilled manual workers, another 25 per cent were in secretarial/clerical occupations and 15 per cent in professional or technical posts. The turmoil of emergent independent African states in the 1950s, with the attendant Africanization programmes, made it impossible for them to remain and many, particularly those who had been employed in the public sector and were therefore most immediately and powerfully affected, migrated to Britain in the mid-1960s.

The experience of being twice migrants had a number of significant effects on their social and economic trajectory following their settlement in Britain (Bachu, 1985). She summarizes these as follows: They

a) were already part of an established community in East Africa, where they had developed considerable community skills prior to migration,
b) moved from urban East Africa to urban Britain, having been concentrated in a handful of towns in East Africa,
c) were mainly public sector workers,
d) were technically skilled because of early recruitment policies [in Africa],
e) despite their absence from India for over seventy years and the lack of home orientation, have maintained many of the values and traditions they migrated with in the early twentieth century,
f) have arrived in Britain with considerable command over mainstream skills (e.g. language, education, familiarity with urban institutions and

bureaucratic processes) and also a certain amount of capital which makes them relatively prosperous.

Further significant variations from the norms of the settlement process experienced by other South Asian communities were that they arrived in Britain as complete families whilst their sojourn in Africa had, as it were, insulated them from India and thus, for them, there was no myth of return. Their arrival in Britain was never perceived as a transient episode, the means to an end which was a return to India where they would be reunited with their people. They arrived in Britain as permanent settlers. This factor, combined with those listed above, powerfully affected the way they adapted to their new circumstances.

A feature of other minority community settlement — and here we are not referring exclusively to South Asian groups but to all new arrivals — is their tendency to form concentrations in particular areas. This did not apply to the East African Asians. They have not gone through the phase of living in inner-city areas and then dispersing to the suburbs with increasing affluence. They tended to disperse on arrival and although large numbers are to be found in London, they are also to be found in most of the larger cities in Britain. For many, this was made easier by the fact that they arrived with financial resources which made it unnecessary for them to buy inexpensive inner-city housing and enabled them to acquire middle-class suburban houses immediately.

Nor do they feel the need to live close to relatives and Bachu (1985) cites examples of the way that families and members of families setting up independent households deliberately distance themselves by some miles from each other. The reason given by her for this dispersal is worth noting.

> They say that they prefer to maintain a distance because they are in this way not involved in the petty quarrels of related families and can therefore lead their own individual lives without their behaviour being monitored by kinsmen.

The comparison here between the East African Asians and the Bangladeshis is so sharp as scarcely to require being made. It may be argued that this is yet another aspect of the lack of the myth of return. For other minority communities it is of extreme importance that family structures and relationships, the behaviour of their members towards each other and between families are maintained along traditional lines to make return possible. For the East African Asians, this control exercised by a 'home' community does not exist. They therefore enjoy a greater freedom to make individual decisions in relationship to British society.

However, it should not be thought that they therefore live isolated lives: the impact of the previous experience in East Africa, the highly developed network of communications between individuals and families which has survived that experience, and the large number of functions which bring them together, ensure a sense of shared community in spite of geographical dispersal. It may also be that their arrival as complete families is significant in this connexion. It meant that, unlike other minority communities, there was from the beginning a natural balance between the sexes and a normal age structure. This, in turn meant that normal social life within and between families could continue without the prolonged dislocation endured by other South Asian communities which adopted the strategy of males (usually heads of households) settling first and then bringing the family over when it was possible and seen to be necessary to do so — often after years of separation. It also meant that there was an immediate pool of suitable marriage partners in Britain which disposed of the problems met by other communities of identifying suitable brides or bridegrooms and then having to overcome the obstacles erected by immigration control.

Despite their apparent (and real) ability to come to terms with and work within British society, East African Sikhs have remained more orthodox in their adherence to Sikhism than many of those who migrated to Britain direct from the Punjab. The absence of ties with the Punjab has not diminished their sense of Sikh identity or reduced the importance of their religious beliefs.

Sikhism contrasts sharply with Islam in the relationship that is encouraged between men and women and the place of women in society. There is no system of purdah. Men and women talk to each other quite freely in public and there is no institutionalized disapproval of women engaging in paid employment. On the contrary, both sexes are expected to become as well educated as their abilities allow and women are encouraged to embark on careers and enjoy success in them.

The Chinese Community

Whilst not all people of Chinese origin now settled in Britain came from Hong Kong, the great majority did and it is for that reason that the following pages are about them. Watson (1977) quoted in Taylor (1987) suggests that approximately 70 per cent of the Chinese in Britain are Cantonese from the New Territories and a further 20 per cent are Hakka, with the remainder from the north, mostly from Taiwan and Singapore.

Hong Kong became a British Crown Colony as part of Britain's attempts to expand trade with China which started in the eighteenth century. Following the first Opium War of 1832–42, Hong Kong Island was ceded by the Treaty of Nanking in 1843. Following the Second Opium War (1858–60) Britain acquired part of the Kowloon Peninsula and Stonecutters Island and in 1898, the Convention of Peking leased a further 365 square miles north of Kowloon, known as the New Territories, for 99 years.

The majority of the population is Cantonese but there is a substantial population of Hakka and until relatively recently these two groups existed as separate communities, though intermarriage is now not unknown. There is also a third group, Hokklo and Tan Ka boatmen who live and work aboard in the many harbours.

Hong Kong is officially bilingual — Cantonese and English — but Taylor

(1987) suggests that nearly nine out of ten cited Cantonese as their first language with 25 per cent of the population aged ten and over able to understand English.

Unlike other Asian groups, many of whom can be identified with and identify themselves by their religion, at least seven major religions are practised in Hong Kong. It is in the blending of these various religions or philosophies (or some of them) which is distinctively Chinese. According to Ladlow (n.d.) many, especially those from the New Territories, adhere to the traditional Chinese religion. This is a mixture of ancestor worship and polytheism, animism, and geomancy, which together influence and are influenced by Confucianism, Taoism and Buddhism.

Confucius was more of a philosopher than a prophet and based his teachings on the concept of *li* — a respectful attitude towards ones's ancestors and fellow men. His followers developed an increasingly refined sense of family through a carefully worked out hierarchy of family relationships.

> Most important was the father-son relationship, the son being expected to serve, to respect and at all times to defer to the father . . . Ancestor worship was the religion which gave strength and supernatural sanction to the family . . . In this way, everyone's position in this life and the after-life was rigidly circumscribed and made subject to the greater welfare of the family unit. (Baker, 1981)

Thus the family is made central to the Chinese culture — more important than either the individual or the community.

Similarly, Taoism (Tao means literally 'the way') advocates a submission to nature, preaching humility, compassion and the requiting of good for evil.

To complicate matters further, Hong Kong also has a substantial Christian community which, from the early days of Hong Kong's development, played an important role in providing educational and medical facilities. Many Chinese immigrants to Britain may well have had contacts with Christianity through schools, hospitals and clinics. Thus, particularly through its educational provisions, Christianity has become increasingly a middle-class religion, attractive to the young people who benefited from it (Taylor, 1987). There are also Hindu, Sikh and Jewish communities in Hong Kong. Thus there are some 600 churches and chapels in Honk Kong with approximately 466,500 Christians, 30,000 followers of Islam, 10,000 Hindus, 3,000 Sikhs and a Jewish community of about 1,000 people (Hong Kong Govt, 1984).

Chinese immigration began in the nineteenth century when single males came to the UK, mainly as seamen and settled in the major ports, chiefly Liverpool and London. The build-up of settlers was slow and the 1901 census suggested that there were only 545 Chinese people in the whole country. Numbers built up steadily at first until immigration increased more rapidly after World War II, with settlers coming mainly from Hong Kong. Until the late 1960s most of these migrants were men. Ng (1968) found that many intended, ultimately, to return. They worked hard, remitted money to their families with whom they kept in close touch through the exchange of letters and newspapers, and planned for their retirement to their villages. However, by the 1970s, as a result of the 1968 Commonwealth Immigration Act which required that children were accompanied by their mothers, increasing numbers of women and children were being brought over to reunite the families. This change was accelerated by increasing worries about the position of Hong Kong with respect to mainland China and by the increasingly severe immigration controls that were being put through parliament. Garvey and Jackson (1975) quote the estimates of a Parliamentary Select Committee that some 1,600 Chinese children were entering the country each year.

Thus the Swann Report (DES, 1985) suggests that some 80 per cent of all Chinese resident in the UK had arrived in the previous twenty years. Chinese immigration has declined in line with other ethnic minority communities since the late 1970s and the most recent reliable estimate of their total number of approximately 100,000 dates from the 1981 census. It is at least possible, however, that a major influx of Hong Kong Chinese will result from the present government's attempt to stabilize the Hong Kong community by guaranteeing right of abode to 50,000 heads of households in 1997.

If this offer is taken up on a large scale it could mean an addition of some 200–250,000 people to the present Chinese community in Britain — effectively more than doubling its present size. More significant than the simple numbers involved, however, would be the nature of the new settlers. The criteria by which they are to be selected ensure that they will be predominantly young, skilled, financially secure, well-educated and competent in English, with a clearly defined self-image of themselves as members of the professional/managerial class. Such a group would contrast sharply with the present community whose corporate history has been very different.

In one of the earliest studies of the Chinese community in Britain, Ng (1968) traces their historical background from the nineteenth century days of sailors through to the era of Chinese laundries and the present day restaurant trade. He shows how, with the rise in numbers of Chinese seeking employment away from shipping, many became involved in the laundry business which he characterizes as useful but dirty work, unwanted by the British and requiring little capital. We would like to stress the importance of this perception by the Chinese of a niche within the British economy where they could operate independently without competing for jobs or capital with indigenous white workers. It was, as Ng suggests, the start of a 'symbiotic, customer-waiter relationship' which was reproduced when, with the collapse of the laundry business following the introduction of the launderette and the home washing machines in the 1950s, they found another solution in their quest for social and economic independence in the development of the restaurant trade.

With the end of rationing Britain wanted more restaurants. The comparatively highly-paid jobs encouraged more Chinese to emigrate and escape the poverty of their rural home life. Until the Commonwealth Immigration Act (1962) there was little to stop Chinese from entering the country and most of those who came did so to work in a restaurant that was very probably owned, or part-owned by a relative. It was the classic example of chain migration in which men settled and started businesses and then were able to recruit willing employees from their families. In this way the businesses could grow with no help being needed from outside their own community. In the early days of the development of the restaurant business, many were actually cooperatives with the starting capital made up of contributions from five or more settlers who then worked in it and recruited labour from Hong Kong. The newly-arrived recruits slept in dormitories and worked in the restaurant.

The second stage of the process was the development of the 'take-away' shops. During the 1970s many fish shops were taken over by Chinese families and converted to 'take-aways' in response to the increasing demand by the public for more exotic food and for service at times when the traditional fish shop was closed. This development also had consequences for the distribution of Chinese families. No 'take-away' owner wanted his premises to be too close to another so the families dispersed through cities and towns and into surrounding villages, wherever there were suitable locations, and set up in business.

Evidence of this dispersal comes not only from common observation but from other sources. Hammond (1990), in a survey of languages spoken by Manchester school children, found that there were only four primary and four secondary schools out of a sample of 200 in which there were more than ten Chinese-speaking pupils.

The economic independence resulting from identifying catering as a niche within the service industry, however admirable in the abstract, carried with it severe penalties in practice. It meant that they had virtually no contact with British society except in a customer relationship, and this only for a few. One result, according to the Nuffield Report (1980), was that fewer than 10 per cent of them learned any English at all. Another was that Chinese families were not only isolated from their English neighbours because of their long and unsocial hours of work and lack of English language skills, but their wide geographical dispersal meant that it was difficult for them to create any real sense of community amongst themselves.

This lack of sense of community was perhaps accentuated by the nature of their religious beliefs. Unlike the South Asian groups, no temples or places of organized worship were built which would bring them together at regular intervals. Moreover, Taylor, reviewing the work of Ng (1968), Clough and Quarmby (1978) and Simsova and Chinn (1982), concludes that there has been a decline in religious practices associated with traditional Chinese religion and 'that the Chinese who do have religious beliefs are likely to be associated with the Christian church, usually an evangelical denomination.' This would seem to coincide with our own findings.

It is this geographical dispersal through indigenous communities which is often cited as the reason for the 'invisibility' of the Chinese presence in Britain. Other recent settlers have started by forming dense local concentrations so that, even though in numerical terms they were not significantly larger than the

Chinese, they have been much more visible. To this invisibility through dispersal should be added their natural independence, their wish to avoid trouble and hence lose face, and their low profile because of the economic niche in which so many flourish. These characteristics have led to their being less noticed and hence, as seems likely, to a reduction in overt discrimination.

There are, however, a number of countervailing factors which may mitigate this sense of families living in isolation. There is a powerful sense of Chineseness that grows from the importance of the family in its immediate and extended form, both as contemporaries and ancestors; a sense of continuity with the past and oneness with the present that enables each Chinese person to carry with him or herself a powerful cultural identity.

Another, and increasingly significant factor, has been the development in recent years in Liverpool and Manchester of substantial community centres. In Manchester in 1979 the Chinese Cultural Centre was inaugurated and provides a social gathering place for some 5,000 Chinese each week located in a district of the city largely given over to their community needs. A wide range of activities is available including language classes, martial arts, painting and calligraphy. Such a Centre suggests a determination by the Manchester Chinese to maintain their culture and the numbers attending — particularly those studying in language classes — make success seem likely. It may also indicate that the community has come to recognize that return is unlikely and that their culture can only be retained by this conscious effort of communal will. How second- and third-generation settlers will accommodate to the dominant culture can only be a matter of conjecture.

The Afro-Caribbean Community

The West Indies is a general term for a group of islands, which, together with some mainland territories extend for some 2,000 miles in the Caribbean Sea. Many, though far from all, were included as part of Britain's colonial territories and of these, Jamaica, Trinidad and Tobago, Barbados and Guyana are the lands from which the majority of people of Caribbean origin now in Britain can trace their origins. As an area of great cultural complexity, the Caribbean has attracted the interest of many anthropologists and much has been written about the impact of the sugar plantations and the slave trade with which they were associated on the culture and lives of their inhabitants. It is, however, generally agreed that the islands and people of the West Indies are far from homogeneous groupings.

In spite of the complexity there is general agreement in the literature about some broad distinctions that can be made. The peoples of these islands have a diversity of origin though the majority seems to be of African extraction. There are, however, substantial numbers from the East Indies, particularly in Trinidad and Guyana where they form half the populations. This variation in origin is reflected in the social class system and in their distinct and different family patterns.

One of the distinct and enduring, central and influential features of West Indian life is the mother-dominated family. Edith Clark's *My Mother who Fathered Me* (1957) remains probably the most detailed anthropological study of Jamaican family life, dealing as it does with aspects of land tenure, marriage, sex and procreation, household organization and the development of kinship roles. The extended family network centred on the mother or grandmother is shown to be the traditional pattern.

The pattern of their migration to Britain is of longer duration and more complex than many other groups. According to Walvin (1984) *The Gentleman's Magazine* of 1764 asserted that there were 20,000 black people in London alone. Their numbers probably increased until the early part of the nineteenth century when they declined with the ending of the slave trade and Britain's loss of interest in the West Indies.

Towards the end of the nineteenth century the numbers of black people arriving and settling began to increase again. This was partly the result of the arrival of increasing numbers of African and West Indian students to study in British universities, but much more to the black sailors who arrived, and stayed, in ports such as Cardiff and Liverpool.

With the beginning of World War I, Britain assumed that its colonial peoples would rally to the flag. It is perhaps extraordinary that they did and Prime Minister Asquith received a telegram: 'Do not worry England, Barbados is behind you.' A West Indian Regiment was formed and before the end of the war more than 15,000 men joined it from most of the Caribbean islands (Walvin, 1985). The outbreak of World War II produced a similar response. By the end of hostilities, some 8,000 West Indians had joined the services.

As may well be understood, the great majority of Afro-Caribbeans coming to and settling in Britain until 1944 had been men. It was in the immediate post-war period that men were accompanied by wives and children. As with other ethnic groups mentioned in this chapter, their decision to come to Britain was partly accounted for by push and partly by pull. Bagley (1977) suggests that many left to escape the rigid social stratification which prevented people of African origin from rising in the educational and occupational system. Taylor (1981), in her review of life in the Caribbean, concludes that it was poverty, the drift towards the towns, increasing unemployment and a growing population which made the option to emigrate attractive. Britain was an obvious destination since its need for people to work in its factories was well-advertised and West Indians from British territories had a legal right of entry until the 1962 Immigrants Act. In Jamaica, a network of travel agencies came into being throughout the island which even offered credit facilities for those unable to find the cash. The Barbadian authorities provided loans and assistance to make the journey possible. Organizations such as London Transport sent out recruiting teams.

West Indians in the UK represent nationals from virtually all the English-speaking Caribbean territories. In any one city, or area of West Indian settlement, migrants from a range of islands are likely to be found. Whilst the heterogeneity of these communities is partly due to horizontal stratification and cleavages based on island or country of origin, the most significant variation in terms of adaptation is that of socio-economic class.

More than half the West Indians in Britain live in the Greater London area and the major proportion of the remainder live in the Midland cities of Birmingham, Wolverhampton, Manchester, Nottingham and Leicester. In spite of the wide range of occupational skills they brought with them, the labour demands of post-war Britain was for people to work in factories, transport, hospitals and other services. Regardless of previous occupations, it was these jobs that the West Indians largely filled. In this they may be distinguished from those who elected to go to the United States and Canada. There the over-all pattern of the occupational distribution of West Indians is skewed towards the more highly-educated white-collar or skilled worker category, whereas in Britain it is weighted towards the blue-collar skilled worker. Therefore, the larger proportion of West Indians in North America are middle class or have middle-class orientations, as compared with the situation in Britain.

The heterogeneity of the United States in terms of race and ethnicity contrasts with the relative homogeneity of the British situation. Despite Canada's considerable ethnic diversity, it has traditionally been a predominantly white population, and until the 1960s, had made every effort to maintain that character.

Two essential aspects are evident in the characteristics of West Indian adaptation in Britain: the re-defining of original migration goals to focus on success in the adopted country rather than on the return home, and the reliance on support groups and the reinforcement of group identity almost as a prerequisite of adaptation. Increasingly, this adaptation brought about a change in the roles that the immigrants assumed. The once highly-demanded contribution to the labour force was no longer seen to be transient or confined to the original occupations. Instead, the West Indian community began to be seen as permanent. Moreover, hostility shown towards them precipitated and cemented group solidarity, even across island cleavages, and has generally encouraged reliance upon their own communities for recognition and status. Thus in London alone, there are some forty formally constituted West Indian Associations listed and many more exist in other cities.

Unlike most of the later settlers from South Asia, those from the Caribbean had the advantage of understanding and being understood in English. To that might be added that many were Christian. Thus they were far nearer in language and culture of the white indigenous population of Britain than people from South Asia. In spite of these advantages, all the evidence shows that the high hopes the original settlers brought with them of social acceptance and economic advancement were disappointed. It might be asked why this was so.

Two theories have been advanced. We would stress that these theories apply equally to ethnic minority communities from South Asia as well as those from the Caribbean. One theory concentrates on racism and discrimination as an explanation and the other on the British class structure. The two are not mutually exclusive. Rex and Tomlinson (1979) in their study of Handsworth in Birmingham sought to discover something of the relationship between Asian and West Indian people to the British class structure. Their disturbing conclusion was that the black population had not been absorbed into the white working class and seemed unlikely to be absorbed in the foreseeable future. In fact, they concluded, they formed an under-class, disadvantaged by comparison with the white working-class in housing, employment and education. The black population is thus placed in a structurally different location and suffers from the *additional* disadvantage because of the hostility directed at them by much of white society. Abercrombie *et al.* (1988) sum up the position as follows, and we would generally agree with them:

> . . . one cannot counterpose the class and racism models of ethnic disad-vantage. A proper explanation has to employ both, even if there is room for argument about the weight to be placed on each factor. The mecha-nisms of the class structure create positions — jobs — which are filled by ethnic minorities, originally entering the country as migrant workers. Racism and its associated discriminatory practices are part of the ex-planation of the way in which black workers fill the worst jobs. Any cor-rection of ethnic disadvantage, therefore, has to focus both on racism and the mechanism of class disadvantage.

Chapter 4

Partners and Partnerships

The Sports Council in Britain is a Government-funded body and the key player in a network made up of other organizations, all concerned, in one way or another, with sport and physical recreation. Those in this network include the governing bodies of sport, the Central Council for Physical Recreation, the National Coaching Foundation and there are many others. Perhaps most importantly from our point of view, the Sports Council can, and often does, powerfully influence the way that local authority leisure departments see their responsibilities. Although it has considerable financial resources, they fade into insignificance by comparison with most of the organizations it does business with. Its power derives in part from its relationship with Government but more from the regard for the expertize and professionalism of its officers held by those with whom they work.

It achieves its ends by a complex set of partnerships with statutory and voluntary bodies concerned with sport and recreation. Since partnership lies at the heart of its strategy, it seemed appropriate to review current policies and practices in the local authorities of Greater Manchester to see how nearly they accorded with the Sports Council's policy in their documentation and practices.

It is hardly necessary to make the point that partnerships only function effectively when partners have established common goals and are equally willing to adopt agreed practices which will lead to those goals being achieved. Where issues arose during the course of the study relating to statements from the Sports Council's own policy, we include those statements as part of the review. It may be argued, of course, that the ten local authorities that make up Greater Manchester could be untypical both in their policies and the ways they put them into practice. In the absence of a nationwide survey there can be no certainty either way. We can only express our opinion, which is that our experience would be substantially replicated by a similar exercise conducted over a comparable area.

Documentary Evidence

In 1989 letters were sent to the chief executives and the heads of leisure departments of ten local authorities in the North-West explaining our interest and asking for policy statements and any secondary documentation, such as codes of practice, that might derive from them. Some documentation was received from all ten authorities. Nine were able to supply formal policy statements and one supplied minutes of meetings within the authority which demonstrated a keen awareness of the need for a policy and indicated that it was actively seeking to formulate one which would not only be a statement of intent but would also incorporate codes of practice leading to its effective implementation.

Employment

The Sports Council set up a Joint Staff-Management Working Party in 1986 to review the Council's policy and procedures in relation to equal opportunities, and it noted that the policy statement then in force was as follows:

> The Sports Council is committed to the development of positive policies to promote equal opportunities in employment.

> The aim of its policy is to ensure that no applicant for employment or existing member of staff receives less favourable treatment on the grounds of sex, creed, colour, race, social background, physical disability, ethnic or national origins or is disadvantaged by conditions or requirements which cannot be shown to be justified. The principle applies in respect of all conditions of work.

> The Council gives full and fair consideration to applications for employment from all eligible persons having regard to their particular aptitudes, ability, qualifications and fitness for work. Selection criteria and procedures are constantly under review to ensure that individuals are selected, promoted and treated on the basis of their relevant merits and abilities. (Equal Opportunities Working Party: First Report, 1986)

The Working Group noted that there had not been any programme of action taken by the Council to 'translate this policy into reality'. There had been no review of criteria and procedures to ensure that they did not result in indirect discrimination and that no action had been taken to develop 'positive policies'.

A survey by the Working Party showed that there was a serious under-representation of people from ethnic minority groups within the organization as a whole and in its central and regional offices. This raised levels of awareness within the Sports Council and was followed by a document entitled *Sports Council Recruitment Policy and Procedures* (1990) which set out in some detail the measures proposed to achieve greater equality of opportunity in employment. Some initiatives in this document — the intention to see how responses to advertisements from disadvantaged groups might be encouraged and the provision that all members of interviewing panels should receive training in interview skills and equal opportunities — were welcome steps in the right direction.

There were, however, a number of reservations we have to record. Firstly, although there was reference to the need to develop 'positive policies' in the Working Party's First Report (and we assume this to mean positive *action* policies), the 1990 document made little provision for this in the procedures it proposed. For example, although the Working Party's Report showed serious under-representation of people from ethnic minority groups, the 1990 document does not suggest that targets should be set for the employment of people from ethnic minorities. Secondly, the use of job descriptions and person specifications as key instruments in recruitment and selection procedures can, and does, actually militate against the success of positive action policies unless the specifications are drafted with positive action as a firmly established prerequisite. There is a danger that the expectations of the person responsible for drafting them will result in specifications that lead to the appointment of candidates who conform to the existing culture of the organization. This danger is particularly acute when the job in question has fallen vacant as the result of the resignation or promotion of the existing post-holder. Thirdly, there is no specific reference to ethnic minority groups in the aims identified as those which the Council accepts as its responsibility to promote. There was a recognition that it should encourage 'disadvantaged groups to take advantage of opportunities' and it may be that the word 'disadvantaged' was intended to include them. However, we believe that a clear distinction should be made between people who are disadvantaged and those who are the victims of discrimination. Men and women may be disadvantaged in a number of ways and it may be held that those who suffer from discrimination are disadvantaged thereby. However, we would suggest that this confuses two quite separate sets of people: those who are disadvantaged by physical, psychological or mental disability, by poverty, by family circumstances or for some other cause and those who are disadvantaged for no other reason than that they are of ethnic minority origin. It is, we believe, unhelpful in policymaking to confuse these two categories since the strategies required to overcome the differing forms of 'disadvantage' have nothing in common. Fourthly, there appeared to be no provision for monitoring initial applications for ethnicity and no clear indication as to the use that would be made of the records of those not invited for interview. In the absence of ethnic monitoring of applicants, data from which is used to test the effectiveness of the procedures adopted, there is no mechanism by which progress towards equality of opportunity can be measured.

Employment Policies

Before proceeding further we should explain that the policy documents and the subsequent interviews with officers of local authorities were obtained on the understanding that no organization or person would be identified in any subsequent publication.

The major emphasis of all local authorities was on equality of opportunity in employment. Typically they contained sentiments such as:

. . . it is the policy of the Council to ensure:

1   That all employees are recruited, trained and promoted on the basis of ability, the requirements of the job and similar objective and relevant criteria.

2   That no job applicant or employee receives less favourable treatment on the grounds of sex, marital status, race, colour, religion, nationality, ethnic or national origin, or is disadvantaged by conditions or requirements which cannot be shown to be justified.

Positive discrimination will be supported only in those areas where it is agreed by representatives of the Council and employees that it is in the interests of individual employees or groups of employees of the Council to overcome special personal disadvantages.

and,

The picture of the Council's workforce (excluding education and direct works operatives) . . . demonstrates beyond question the need for the Council's equal opportunities policy and the need for concerted determined action to redress the imbalances and inequalities in the employment position of women, black people and disabled people.

All the other authorities had published policies which had equality of employment as their objective and all made specific references to race or ethnic origin.

Service Delivery

The Sports Council . . . will

Encourage local authorities, voluntary and commercial sports organizations to adopt positive policies that encourage the provision of opportunity for sport and recreation that embrace the specific needs of ethnic communities.

As we understood it, the Council had adopted a two-pronged strategy for achieving these ends. Individual officers in regional offices, particularly, but not exclusively, those with responsibilities for promoting work with ethnic minority groups, were to seek to influence local authorities and other organizations by encouraging Sports Development Officers and Action Sport staff to focus their efforts on increasing participation by ethnic minorities. Other methods included mounting demonstration projects and giving preference to proposals which furthered the Council's objectives. At national level, governing bodies of sport were being required, as a condition of continued support by the Council, to supply development plans for their sport. We were informed that these development plans had concentrated in the first instance on strategies and measures to improve performance and to achieve excellence. We saw no reason why, in future, these development plans should not be required to show how the governing bodies intended to further the Council's policies generally and those relating to ethnic minorities in particular.

We have to say that most local authority policy statements had little or nothing to say about how, or to whom, their services were to be delivered. We believe this was largely due to a lack of data which could have supported decision-making. One authority was quite open about this:

> The Council recognizes that in certain respects it has an imprecise understanding of the extent to which its existing service provision and employment policies meet the needs of the community. The Council will institute a programme of work to improve its awareness. If it is demonstrated by review that need/disadvantage is associated with geographical area, gender, age, etc., the Council will consider opportunities for alleviating problems. It is acknowledged that some of its policies and practices may need to be modified, or new policies and practices introduced. *The Council accepts that one consequence is likely to be a programme of positive action in an endeavour to achieve equality of choice and access to services for disadvantaged groups.* (Our emphasis)

It included the following statement on service delivery.

> Within the overall resource constraints the Council is committed to meeting needs and offering appropriate opportunities in service provision and employment for all members of the community and will work towards an improved awareness of the needs of groups with particular disadvantages.

> Within the Council's perception of the total needs and views of the community, it recognizes that all sections of the community have an equal right to the maintenance of distinctive cultural, linguistic and religious identities.

Another authority used data from the 1981 census to point up the size, distribution and age profiles of its (largely Asian) ethnic minority population on which it based the following observations:

> [We already have] a substantial minority population and this population is growing faster than the indigenous majority . . .

> What do these figures mean for future Council policies? Should we assume that over time the existing cultural differences will blur as groups become assimilated into the population at large, or should we plan on the assumption that differences will remain?

Other authorities have addressed this question and the general conclusion has been that assimilation, if it happens at all, will take several generations to accomplish. A people's culture is not a passing fad; it is a question of deeply held belief, a part of the way in which people see the world and see themselves. Adverse economic or social conditions tend to intensify these beliefs as minorities are forced to depend on one-another for mutual support. Equally important, people see their own culture as something natural and correct, and feel they have something important to offer to people of other cultures.

If this view is correct, then LAs should plan service delivery on a pluralistic basis. Services should be equally available to anyone who needs them, and if the service is uniform in style then groups who do not conform to that uniformity will be at a disadvantage.

Later, as part of its Corporate Policy Statement, it had the following to say:

The Council . . . commits itself to taking all the necessary steps within its power as an employer, as a major provider of services within the area, and as a major influence on public opinion, to bring about the conditions where good race relations are best able to flourish. In particular it commits itself to a policy of encouraging equal opportunity, to reducing racial disadvantage, and to eradicating racial discrimination.

It recognizes also that since [the authority] now has both a multi-racial and multi-cultural population, all sections of the community are entitled to maintain their distinctive loyalties of culture, language, religion and custom.

The document then set out the means by which it proposed to attain those ends and these included the maintenance of ethnic records, the improvement of communication between the Council and ethnic minority communities through the creation of a Minorities Joint Consultative Committee and the encouragement of community development and self-help initiatives within the minority communities.

We repeat, however, that such statements on service delivery were unusual. Whilst all placed a heavy emphasis on the need for equality in employment, few related their responsibility for the provision of services to the needs of their ethnic minority communities.

Leisure Services Departments

Representatives of leisure services departments said that they were bound by the policies of the authority and responsive to the policy priorities of the Sports

Council. Only three had policy documents of their own which covered either employment or service delivery. Of those that did, one provided a good example of the way that knowledge obtained from a study of the needs of local people could lead to informed policymaking.

The Council had conducted a major survey of the Bangladeshi community and the leisure services department was in the very early stages of developing a recreation strategy document in response to that report. We are grateful to the officer responsible for this development for allowing us to quote from the first draft of this document.

Under an objective expressed as 'The service will reflect the rich cultural mixture of the borough's population' are the following statements:

To achieve this, the department will:

Seek to employ a [target percentage] of minority community members within its client and development sections and encourage any recreation contractor operating on its behalf within the [authority] to do so.

Continue to run varied training packages aimed specifically at minority community groups in order to address barriers to participation, raise awareness of related issues and increase employment potential.

Through the leisure contract specifications ensure that the programming of leisure contract resources is sympathetic to minority community members.

Set out specific aims of major resources identifying clearly their roles in [providing for] certain community areas.

Published information advertising and promoting the recreational service in [community] languages.

Seek to employ within the community development team an officer or staff with specific responsibility for minority community issues.

Under another objective, 'Continue to identify non-participant groups within the community and seek to remove prohibitive barriers' the intentions (among others) are to:

Operate a team of Action Sport Officers with clearly-defined target groups and work programmes.

Support a network of voluntary or casual paid sports leaders operating through the Action Sport Team with the community.

Continue to foster partnership ventures with such statutory agencies as the Sports Council . . .

Even in an early draft stage, we would single out a policy statement such as this as an example that other leisure departments might wish to use as a model. We would particularly draw attention to the following aspects of the statement.

- Implicit throughout is the recognition that the strategy of *targeting* defined groups *implies positive action* towards them.
- It recognizes the need for policy decisions on employment *and* service delivery.
- The *focus* is on *people* rather than on facilities or activities. It recognizes that, for low- or non-participants, priority must be given to making contacts, developing understanding and engaging in social (as much as recreational) education.
- It recognizes the need to set *specific targets* for employment.
- It recognizes the need to *relate resources to users*.
- It proposes to develop teams (including voluntary and part-time staff) to operate with the community.
- It recognizes the importance of *appropriate community languages* in promoting activities and increasing awareness of sport and recreation.

Another leisure department had carried out an ethnic audit of their own staff and compared the results with their local population. As a result:

Steps will be taken to ensure that employment opportunities for seasonal and temporary staff are targeted in a positive way to welcome applications from Asian/Afro-Caribbean origins ... As for the 'pool' of casual staff, similar steps will be taken.

In terms of service delivery,

As a component of a marketing strategy the Action Sport Unit to continue to market services to targeted low-participation groups including ethnic minorities, women and disabled people.

We should add that, although there was an absence of policy commitment by leisure departments in other authorities, they were not necessarily unaware of the needs of ethnic minorities. Indeed, much excellent work was being done. However, officers seeking to target ethnic minority groups were operating in a formal policy vacuum.

Grant Aid by the Sports Council

Although grant aiding organizations is only a part — and not a major part — of the Sports Council's activities, we see it as of real significance. By ensuring that its partners are aware of its priorities in allocating grants it can have a major influence on their thinking and practices.

Over the period of our study, the North-West region's policies and practices were being substantially amended. These changes arose from a continuing debate within the organization which sought to bring into alignment its development programme and its funding policies. The changes were the result of the targeting philosophy adopted by the Sports Council which has led to the adoption of an increasingly proactive stance. Another factor in the debate was the Sports Council's increasingly clear perception of itself as a regional agency operating at a strategic level. Thus, in the period 1990–91, revenue grant aid was given to projects which satisfied at least one of the following criteria:

- Provides an innovative approach in response to changing circumstances.
- Seeks to establish and demonstrate good practice in a particular field.
- Provides the opportunity to disseminate good practice and sound management advice.
- Seeks to raise awareness and influence attitudes to assist the removal of barriers affecting participation by people from target groups in sport.

In addition, there was a move away from large numbers of small grants to individual clubs towards increased funding for large strategic schemes. This may be illustrated by the fact that between 1989–90, the region grant-aided 178 development schemes and in 1990–91 the number of schemes aided fell to 48. This move resulted from the recognition that, increasingly, staff resources were being consumed in dealing with small schemes so that their real cost was being inflated out of all proportion to their value. Consequently, small clubs were increasingly referred to their local authorities as their normal resource. As part of this strategy, the Sports Council was helping to fund posts for Sports Development Officers at Principal Officer level within selected local authorities. Five were already in post and two more were being negotiated. It was believed that they would make a substantial improvement to sports development in those authorities.

The criteria for capital grants for facilities had also changed from a mechanistic approach dominated by fairly arbitrary definitions of standards to a recognition that grants should essentially be sports development-led. This change had been facilitated by the introduction of a computerized facilities planning model which lent itself more flexibly to the region's general approach. Interviews and discussions with regional officers strongly suggested that the new approach would be one of greater discrimination, supporting those schemes which clearly related to the Sports Council's objectives, on a three-year rolling plan, incorporating a systematic monitoring programme.

The increase in alignment between policy, practice and mechanisms by which funding was allocated seemed likely to benefit those groups targeted by the Sports Council. Certainly, the change in emphasis to the users and potential users of facilities was a welcome one. However, it was clearly going to be some years before the benefits of that change would work through. Moreover, the extent to which the changes would benefit ethnic minority groups was unclear. Our view was that too much depended on the relationship between the Sports Council and its partners, particularly the local authorities and schools who, as our findings show, were their major providers. In this connexion the Sports Council's training programmes provided for, among others, local authorities and school governors, took on a particular significance.

Finance for sports facilities.
In its advice for those considering applying for grants or loans, the Sports Council writes:

> Although the Sports Council imposes no fixed upper limit on the level of grant and/or loan it can offer towards the approved/eligible cost of a project, funds are restricted and applicants will be expected to demonstrate financial commitment appropriate to the project.

As innumerable surveys have shown, ethnic minority groups are, in general terms, economically disadvantaged by comparison with British norms. We also cite evidence to that effect collected in the course of this study (see, for example, data on the Bangladeshi community in Oldham and more generally in our findings from the questionnaire survey). Thus the effect of making financial requirements which may be seen as entirely reasonable in the context of the majority of British applicants (white, middle class) is indirectly discriminatory when applied to ethnic minority applicants.[1]

We thought it not unreasonable for the Sports Council to require its regional offices to devise appropriate local mechanisms by which ethnic minority groups could bid for small grants — perhaps up to £500 with no lower limit. The financial and other rules governing the award of these grants and the bureaucratic processes involved would be minimal, consistent with the small sums involved. The prime criteria would be that 1) the grants respond to the needs of people from ethnic minority groups and 2) that they are likely to result in increased participation.

Grant aid to local authorities.
Where the Sports Council joins in partnership with a local authority to fund a new facility or extend an existing one, the proportion of its contribution to the whole cost is relatively small. This masks its true significance, which lies in the influence of its implied approval on the minds of members of decision-making bodies within local government. Thus its power to influence events is out of all proportion to its actual financial input. The same considerations apply equally in the case of jointly funded sports development programmes.

Again, it seemed reasonable that the Sports Council should make it a condition of partnership in all such ventures that the local authority adopted criteria employing the same priorities as those which it had developed for itself and were set out in its own documentation.

Monitoring

At the risk of tedious repetition, we re-state our position over monitoring. Formal policy development and institutional goodwill are, of themselves, *useless*. Unless well-conceived and effective monitoring procedures are in place and routinely providing data in a form that can be, and is, used by management as the basis for informed action, formal policy documents are the written expression of empty breath. Moreover, we contend that the policy documents themselves must be quite specific about the means that are to be adopted to achieve the ends they define. Thus the use of words like 'encourage' have little force and no value unless they are supported by statements which make it clear what form the encouragement that is to be given will take and what criteria will be used to evaluate the results of that encouragement.

Probably because of the speed at which the North-West region's policies were changing, up-to-date documentation showing in detail how these were to be achieved, monitored and evaluated were not available. Even though discussions with officers showed that these processes were perceived as part of the routine work of the office, we strongly suggested that they should be documented so as to form part of its formally recognized policy and practice.

Local Authority Monitoring

As we have already observed in this chapter, the local authorities' major emphasis in their policy statements was on employment. It was not altogether surprising therefore, to discover that monitoring procedures, where they existed, addressed the issue of equality of opportunity in employment. We have to record that, in too many cases, promises of monitoring procedures contained in seven of the ten policy documents received, were not carried through. An example of one such read as follows:

> A system shall be developed to enable monitoring to be carried out on ethnic origins, disablement and sex regarding:
> a)   the numbers applying for jobs in each category,
> b)   the numbers shortlishted in each category,
> c)   the numbers employed in each category,
> d)   the numbers leaving in each category,
> e)   the numbers participating in training and staff development,
> f)   the numbers promoted.

At the time of the study, no authority-wide monitoring system had been developed. Some departments or divisions within departments had set up systems, others had not. Where monitoring had been developed it formed part of a general good equal opportunities practice.

Other authorities whose documentation expressed similar intentions were found, on closer inspection, not to have carried them through into practice. In one case it appeared that changes in the political complexion of the Council since the policy statement had effectively made it a dead letter and the actions promised had not been taken. In the course of discussions we were informed that there were no officers within the authority with designated responsibilities for equal opportunities. No monitoring systems had been set up either for employment or service delivery. It was put to us that the current thinking within the authority was that to develop such systems would be contrary to the principles of integration: it would differentiate 'them' from 'us'.

A particularly sad case was that of an authority whose documentation demonstrated a well-developed internal monitoring system. It had adopted a set of categories by which its employees identified their ethnicity. These were: African, Afro-Caribbean, Bangladeshi, black British, Chinese, East African Asian, Indian, Middle East, other black, Pakistani, Vietnamese, Irish, white British and other white.

In the course of a detailed and necessarily lengthy argument supported by statistical evidence from its own monitoring procedures and a sample survey of the total population, their documentation argued the importance of equality targets allied to a timetable for their achievement with recruitment monitoring to establish the effectiveness of the action plans proposed. This led to a conclusion that:

> The council adopt as a formal objective the achievement of 12.5 per cent black employees (as a proportion of the total number of its employees). That there be within the 12.5 per cent the objective of 6.25 per cent black women employees; that this target be reviewed annually.

> The Council adopt an eight-year timescale for the achievement of its objectives for overall representation within the workforce of black people, . . . [and] black women . . .

The eight-year timescale had been arrived at by an analysis of staff turnover within the authority which suggested that such a timescale presented a reasonable and achievable target.

The way this authority had set about the business of righting what it perceived as social injustice seemed admirable. With regret therefore, we record that, in practice, extensive restructuring within the authority and restrictions on recruitment resulting from financial constraints imposed by Government invalidated these calculations. The Council's strategy of restructuring and internal redeployment of staff to meet the financial constraints now enforced have indefinitely postponed any real progress along the course which it had charted towards equality of opportunity in employment.

Where ethnic monitoring *was* employed, the results could be disconcerting. In the latter part of 1989, one authority conducted an audit of its employees by department, by gender, by level of employment and by ethnic origin. It was interesting and instructive to note that fourteen years after the passing of the Race Relations Act (1976) and the Council's original publication of a policy on equality in employment, this audit shows that, if teaching staff were excluded from the calculation, less than 1 per cent of the manual and only 1.23 per cent of its salaried staff were of non-European origin. Also of interest were the results of monitoring the progress of applications for jobs within the authority between August 1988- February 1989. This showed that nearly 4,500 persons of European origin and 180 of non-European origin had applied for jobs. Of the European applicants, 364 or 8 per cent were actually appointed. The figures for non-Europeans were 8 (3 per cent of applicants) actually appointed. It is both fair and instructive to note that this audit resulted in renewed activity on the part of senior officers of the authority with a view to developing employment procedures leading to greater fairness.

There are a number of observations we feel compelled to make.

1)   The Race Relations Act (1976) lays a duty on local authorities:

> Without prejudice to their obligation to comply with any other provision of this Act, it shall be the duty of every local authority to make appropriate arrangements with a view to securing that their various functions are carried out with due regard to the need:
> a)   to eliminate unlawful racial discrimination; and
> b)   to promote equality of opportunity, and good relations, between persons of different racial groups. (Race Relations Act, 1976, s71)

2)   Computer facilities have been available to local authorities which would have made ethnic audits of their staffs possible at any time since 1976.
3)   Failure to do so has denied local authority managers access to data by which they could assess progress towards equality.
4)   Lack of data has also made it impossible for recruitment and selection procedures to be introduced which could be tested through monitoring their outcome and, if necessary, amended so as to bring about equality.
5)   A comparison between the way financial rules are properly enforced through careful financial monitoring, and the general failure to monitor the outcome of equality of opportunity policies through the results of recruitment and selection procedures is as depressing as it is inevitable.

Governing Bodies of Sport

In an attempt to arrive at an assessment of the general level of awareness informing the bodies responsible for governing an array of sporting and recreational activities, a letter of inquiry was sent to seventy-nine of them. Our letter asked for any information they were able to supply on 'policies developed or advice given to affiliated clubs to achieve greater access to people from all ethnic groups.' As is well-known, postal surveys often achieve very low levels of response, so we included the statement that 'it will be assumed that a non-reply will indicate that no policy exists and no advice has been given to affiliated clubs.'

In the event, we received responses from thirty governing bodies. Of these, one was not typical of the rest and supplied a statement of its policy of equal opportunities which was clear and comprehensive. One governing body provided documents which clearly expressed its commitment to equality of opportunity. One of these documents in particular set out its objectives in unequivocal terms. Among its principal objectives were:

1) To promote closer links between the . . . club and its local community,
2) to involve disadvantaged ethnic and minority groups in social and recreational activities.

Three other bodies referred in general terms to having 'policies' for encouraging ethnic minority participation in their sports and pointed with pride to the numbers from ethnic minority groups who participated in them. No policy document was enclosed and we assume that none existed. Common observation supports their claims of attracting substantial numbers of black participants. However, it is possible that other factors are operating to bring about these high levels of participation and we would suggest that included in them are the existence of well-known role models, the association of the sport with the country of ethnic origin or that internationally known teams wholly or largely composed of players from a minority group have been successfully promoted by the media. None the less, the evident pleasure felt by these respondents at being able to point to multi-ethnic participation in their sports was cheering and, as has been demonstrated earlier in this section, the existence of a formal policy does not, of itself, mean anything. Another body referred to the instructions given to its development team which:

have been advised to follow a policy of positive discrimination towards ethnic minority groups in order to encourage newcomers to participate in the sport.

We recognize the need to organize special initial training for some ethnic groups . . .

We believe that this governing body would be the first to admit that few people from any of the minority groups at present participate in its sport and it will be interesting to see if these good intentions can be translated into real achievement.

Another body who positively responded to the question did not refer to any policy decision but wrote:

. . . we strongly support the Sports Council's views in respect of ethnic minorities. We have an extensive programme of development . . . aimed at encouraging this particular group of the population . . . to participate in our sport.

Yet another, which (with reason) claimed that they had 'no problems with the clubs integrating players from ethnic minorities' included a copy of a recent letter from its chairman to all members of the Executive Council which was headed 'Towards greater participation in sport from black and ethnic minorities.' It included the following:

> Increasingly we have to look at what we as a governing body are doing to encourage black and ethnic minorities to take responsibility in sport.
>
> I propose setting up a working party to look at this issue and would welcome any nominations you have. Clearly, we have many players and some coaches but at present no member of Executive or R & G P.

Of the responses we received, this was unique in recognizing that it is crucially important that ethnic minority people should not only be encouraged to participate but also *have an entitlement to power and responsibility in the government of their sport at the highest levels.*

The majority of respondents were quite open in their admissions that they had no policy on encouraging access to their sports by members of ethnic minorities. Of these, many claimed that it was unnecessary since they could point to large numbers of black and/or Asian participants. At an individual level it was hard to disagree with the respondent who wrote:

> [The sport] in general has a very high proportion of inner-city and ethnic minority participants, particularly at elite national and international level.

Or with another who wrote:

> Members of these communities play [the sport] at the highest championship level. Some of the clubs have large numbers of ethnic players. This applies to both male and female players. In addition, many hold administrator and technical posts.

Or another:

> [The sport] I feel, in many ways is a one-off where we have had complete integration for many years, and, with few exceptions, no problems at all. We are now starting to get people from the ethnic minorities coming through as [executives] as well as simply [players]. This is something the Board encourages greatly . . .

There were many more in the same vein.

Responses from governing bodies who had neither policies nor ethnic minority participants were, perhaps understandably, relatively scarce. Of those who did reply, we extract the following two observations.

My personal view is that the lack of participation by ethnic minorities in certain sports is related more to cultural attitudes than to active discrimination.

And,

... at the present time, [the sport] is under-provided ... In practice this means that nearly 75 per cent of ... clubs are full ...

It would be difficult therefore to offer any advice to ... clubs with regard to greater equality of access.

Most respondents in this group wrote to say that their clubs were open to anyone who wanted to play and that there was no discrimination.

One respondent who admitted to having no policy deserves mention. The Secretary to the Association wrote:

We have not at present developed any policies or given advice to our affiliated clubs designed to achieve greater access to people from all ethnic groups. We are still very much at the stage of learning ourselves before really being able to give such advice.

Several of our ... groups in various parts of the country are gaining a little expertise in this field which we will be hoping in due course to share. Certainly in a couple of years we would hope to be able to give a more positive reply to your question.

Oral Evidence

We now move to non-documentary sources of information about the work of the leisure departments. In this part of the section on local authorities as partners we have selected a number of topics that formed a major part of the conversations we recorded with heads of departments or their nominated officers and others. At least one interview was given by officers from all ten of the authorities that make up Greater Manchester. In many cases, two or three contributed their views in the discussion and, in most cases, follow-up interviews were arranged with their colleagues. In all, forty-three interviews were recorded.

Compulsory Competitive Tendering (CCT)

Throughout the period of the study, CCT was an issue that occupied the minds and energies particularly of senior officers in leisure departments. That is not to say that many of them were directly involved in the preparation of the contracts that were to go out to tender. It appeared that many Councils responded to the new legislation by setting up special units to deal with the situation brought about by the Local Government Act on a corporate basis, with the result that those who were responsible for delivering the service were not always closely involved in the response to the challenge. Heads of department were likely to be, but discussions with those towards the sharp end of the service suggested that they had little opportunity directly to influence either the strategies underlying the contracts or the details that were being built into them.

As one officer we interviewed observed:

> There's a vast difference between workspace contracts such as cleaning, refuse collection and grounds maintenance and management contracts such as leisure ... If we use the same model of response to leisure management as we have used to cleaning and refuse collection, we will get into a terrible mess.

So far as CCT's impact on provision for ethnic minorities is concerned, the timing of events means that it was too early to come to any conclusions as to its ultimate impact. In any event, there was great confidence on the part of officers that the leisure departments would, certainly in the first round, win their own contracts. Most echoed the forcibly expressed opinion of one who said:

> ... the Government knows that it's not going to get takers in the North anyway. Who is there? Who is there in the leisure market up here? There isn't anybody. I'm telling you *there is not any body*.

Thus for the immediate future, the authorities' present priorities and practices were seen (by most) to be secure from purely legal constraints, though that is not to say that they were not feeling a wind of change. In the longer term it was suggested that the most likely competition for the authorities would come from their own officers who might go private and bid for the contracts.

In more than one authority, officers were concerned about the generalized effects on what they described as the 'culture' of the department. One of them was very clear that his department was committed to positive action as a matter of mainstream policy. (He was also one of the very few senior officers we interviewed who was prepared to say quite unequivocally that local authority provision was not, could not, and should not be a universal provision but should be particularly targeted at those who most needed it.)

> I don't believe that local authorities are about making provision for everybody, although some local authorities might say that and find it politically unacceptable to say anything else ... I'm saying that I'm providing a service for those people who otherwise would not get it ... In my view, provision is about participation by particular groups ... I'm not competing with the private sector to provide swimming for (for example)

somebody who can afford to go to perhaps a private pool or travel long distances to go to the pool of their choice. If I'm getting, for instance, at a particular pool, hundreds of thousands of people but none of those are Asian ladies, I'm going to be worried about that.

It was in the light of that kind of ethos that he then went on to say of CCT:

... there's the issue of culture, which I think is important. [I feel] that I'm being pushed — and every Council is being pushed — on this line of commercial culture, and that that is what you need in order to be able to compete. Now I don't actually think that's true, and I think it represents commercialism as being efficiency. My worry is that we haven't got a definition of efficiency ...

I'm not too worried about somebody else getting in, I'm worried that the authority uses the *threat* of competitive tendering to alter my employment practices, to alter the culture of my organization so that this kind of caring service culture that I'm trying to develop here gets substituted for a hard, commercial, money-at-all-costs attitude.

This seemed to us a very real cause for concern. If his fears were justified, the effects of CCT could be very damaging to ethnic minorities — and indeed to minority sports — the impact would be rapid and it would not be a necessary consequence of the legislation.

Not all departments of leisure shared the view that it was their business to take positive action in favour of those who needed it most in the community. As one officer put it:

I can understand the logic there. I mean, I can understand that particular viewpoint [but] I'm not so sure that I fully support it. I think an authority, a local authority, a council, has got an obligation to provide for the whole of a community ... There are affluent people in the community, yes, but they shouldn't necessarily be made to join private clubs ... Even the affluent have got a right to choose to use local authority facilities.

Elsewhere the views expressed were essentially that it was the department's job to provide adequate facilities and market the opportunities they afforded.

It was a common perception that the need to draft a contract to put out to tender was concentrating the minds of departments wonderfully. As one officer put it:

Whereas at the moment we are very subjective in our policies towards disadvantaged groups in that, yes, we put them in but we don't do it in any systematic way; it's just, we see the need . . . and we tend to respond to local circumstances . . . So in a way, our response for all disadvantaged groups has been reactive rather than proactive. We've done something when the need has arisen. Now, because of competitive tendering, we're going to have to foresee what provision we will need so that we can write it into the specifications . . .

From another authority, which had been further advanced in its targeting of provision for minority groups before being faced with the demands of CCT, an officer made a similar point but with a different emphasis. He was responding to our statement that a number of officers in other authorities saw some benefit in having to identify their priorities and that this might be good for groups such as ethnic minorities.

I would have to go along with that. Having said that, I've got one reservation. The specification *has* to include specific plans and safeguards for minority groups, or they won't happen . . . Because of the cost; that's the crunch. I mean, one thing that will happen through competition is (I personally think it's not before time either) it is making us look at efficiency, cost effectiveness, and it is *making us* lay down some specific plans . . . I think the burden really does rest fairly and squarely on the authority. If it doesn't do its work properly, everybody in community terms is going to suffer. Because obviously, whether it's an in-house or out-of-house operation, it'll be purely statistically or financially orientated. It'll be numbers through the doors or pounds in the bank. And obviously, the smaller groups, the groups that are more costly to organize, that don't necessarily break even, or whatever, they're going to go by the wayside.

His concern throughout this part of the interview was for the need to protect the arrangements already made for ethnic minority groups and, if possible, improve them through the contract, allied to the belief that if they were not protected, they would lose out and the progress made by the authority in encouraging participation would be nullified.

An officer from one authority with a substantial South Asian population felt that CCT would do little to affect the work he was doing with the community.

Ethnic groups tend not to use our mainline facilities now . . . so really, CCT should have no noticeable effects on present work with ethnic groups.

It was suggested to him that, with the hoped-for success of a recently appointed officer with a special brief to increase ethnic minority participation, in two or three years' time and with an increasing interest, they might find themselves disadvantaged. He remained pretty optimistic.

Yes, that could be the point, when groups have been identified, we've made contact with them and they've become more aware of what's available, CCT could have an effect. Having said that, I think the authority does have control over things like pricing policy . . . that won't change. And it's not envisaged that the booking procedures will be any different. The management of the facilities might be a little bit different, but the management of the facilities as they are already doesn't tend to lean towards sympathy towards ethnic groups — to be quite honest.

We asked him if he would expand on the last statement which he was happy to do.

What I meant was that the actual management of the facilities — the way that the booking systems were operated. As well as that, a lot of information hasn't gone out to ethnic groups in the past — maybe because the managers themselves haven't had the opportunity to get in touch with them. I didn't mean the actual managers themselves, as individuals; I meant management as a system, a structure.

So, while the authority will retain control in ways I've mentioned, it may be that if a private company won the contract, they might well make changes and those changes could be of benefit. Any change might be a change for the better.

The most optimistic view was that of one officer who believed that the contracts could be so written as to ensure that he retained virtually full control of leisure provision within his authority. His argument was that the legislation was intended to ensure the most efficient *management* of the facilities. Therefore, 'That is what I have to put out to competition and that's *all* I will put out to competition.' He would retain control of marketing and promotion and all other activities designed to get people to the centres to do whatever they wanted to do. It would be the contractor's sole job to provide them with the services they demanded once they were in the centres and at prices which he would retain control of. He was, in our view rightly, very concerned that departments in many authorities would draw up contracts that sought to protect the interests of minority groups but which would be so specific that they would restrict any further development. In his words:

[They might say] On a Tuesday night we have run an Asian Ladies swimming session and you're *going to run* an Asian Ladies swimming session . . .

I think that's very difficult and very inflexible. If I've got an Asian Ladies swimming session on a Tuesday night now, am I going to want to have an Asian Ladies swimming session in four years time on a Tuesday night? Might I not also want one on a Sunday morning, or a Wednesday afternoon?

The way I would actually choose to do it is to control every single thing the law allows me to control and essentially have only a works-based contract where all I'm asking the contractor to do is to provide the staff to do exactly what I tell him.

One officer we were able to interview shortly after his authority had had its Community Charge capped at some £300M below its original level had similar views in principle but was concerned about the practical effects of financial constraints.

I've no fears that [the authority] could not produce a tender document or a set of specifications that didn't take due regard to those issues [forms of positive action towards ethnic minorities] because they are central to this Council's commitments . . . What does worry me is the fact that resources will be so reduced, so dramatically reduced . . . to the point where the department starts to lose sight of itself simply because it ceases to exist as a professional unit . . . [Restructuring in an attempt to make economies so that] it's not inconceivable that we, as a department, could be split up into half a dozen and get shelved some-where with no central administration.

It is difficult to predict the long-term effect of CCT. It seemed that different authorities are approaching the issue in different ways and with different expec-tations. However, it was possible to say that one effect was to make leisure departments think hard about their priorities. As our review of local authorities' documentation makes clear, the majority were able to provide us with little in the way of formally expressed policies from which to generate desirable practices under the new management arrangements.

We are not suggesting that good practice is impossible without written policies. It is our experience, however, that policy development can be a learn-ing experience; that the corporate *process* of creating policy works not only by establishing priorities and assessing their resource implications but also (and we would argue, just as importantly) it demands that those participating in the process examine themselves, their predilections and their prejudices. The process also creates a corporate sense of responsibility for seeing that the policy is put into practice.

We suggest also that much depends on the department's historical stance on the nature of the service it should provide: whether it believes it should pro-vide equally for all or preferentially for those who are socially and economically deprived. Clearly, where there has been a history of targeting particular groups because the department has seen its job in terms of social welfare, it is better prepared and more likely to preserve its priorities than one where the approach has been more pragmatic.

Local Management of Schools (LMS)

Whilst, in general, there seemed to be a consensus about CCT and the ability of departments to handle the problem, perceptions of the extent to which provision would be affected by Local Management of Schools, varied substantially from one authority to another.

Some of this variation could be simply accounted for. Some authorities had developed dual-use facilities and made heavy use of facilities within schools. They were in a much less enviable position than authorities which had built public facilities and encouraged schools to make use of them. Those who were optimistic tended to see LMS as potentially good for minority groups, particularly where there was an excess of demand over supply in public facilities.

> Certainly in the mid-week market (Monday to Friday, 5.30 to 10.30) we don't have enough capacity, certainly throughout the winter, to meet all the demand. We turn away bookings, we do turn away block bookings. I would think that because there is an excess of demand over provision at the moment, the schools will be able to tap into that demand and meet it — to their benefit and to the benefit of the communities.

This view was echoed by an officer from another authority who was strongly of the opinion that the long tradition of schools as serving their communities, as well as financial advantages, might well result in greater benefits for the communities they served.

> In [our authority] we had a problem of winning over our colleagues in the education field about issues like shared use. I think [with the development of] LMS, schools will be starting to look at ways in which they can use their resources to better effect. Undoubtedly, one of the ways they will do that is in the area of recreation. Maybe a reason will be for income generation, but I think they will still be governed . . . by the fact they have to be sensitive to the communities they serve. There are no better groups than schools, and particularly primary schools, in terms of sensitivity to the communities they serve.

Others were rather less confident about what would happen. Again, much depended on local circumstances including existing patterns of provision and the perceptions of the responses of the Council's elected members. In one authority with a well-established dual-use system, a central letting system had been in operation for some time. This gave access for established organizations to any facility in the authority.

Now, it has certain principles and philosophies in its own right. They let, for example, to any youth group free. They also let to certain other groups — adult groups — at 25 per cent reductions, if it can be shown that what they are doing is 'educational' or 'beneficial to the community'. And various other concessions can be picked up. Now, question: 'Will those facilities continue to be provided free of charge when that particular school goes independent?'

Now there's two lines of thought here. One is that it can remain on the central letting system and the central letting system will let those premises for the school. It will then subsidize the school for that usage. The other line of thought is 'No it can't'. [The school's] going to have to come out and the governors are going to employ a caretaker, a manager, call it what you want — a Sports Development Officer! — who is going to go out into the community and sell those facilities . . .

I know for a fact, having spoken to colleagues in the education department, it's there. Those are the lines of thought, those are the questions that are being raised and somewhere along the line there will have to be answers to those questions. A lot of it will be politically guided, I'm sure. I mean, some sort of political will will be expressed in relation to this . . . And it could influence the behaviour of the governors, because, obviously, some of the elected members are members of the governing bodies.

In another authority, school-based facilities came under three different sets of arrangements: schools whose facilities were controlled by the leisure department in the evenings and at weekends; other schools, which controlled their own; and a third group whose facilities were hired out centrally by the education department. So, in effect, there were currently in existence three booking systems to get access to school-based facilities. The schools in the first group would come under the control of whoever won the bid for CCT. It was for the second group (defined as community schools) that LMS might have a real significance.

Their charging system is totally different. They charge next to nothing; totally negotiable. If a local community group came along and made a good case, they could have it for a very small charge or even nothing at all. So I think that's where the effect could come in.

At the time of the interview, the authority's Action Sport officer was very much involved in working with ethnic communities in their own centres. However, he accepted that it was quite possible that, in future years, he might well wish to make use of school facilities with them, or encourage them to use these facilities. If, in the meantime, they had moved to pricing policies to maximize income rather than meeting local needs, it could clearly be disadvantageous. Like many others, he felt that much depended on the sympathies of governors and headteachers. Of them he observed:

> Some are convinced that community education is the right way to go. Others may be very much into creating income from their facilities. It may be that, at some stage, groups who can't afford to use [mainstream] facilities and are looking for cheap facilities — it's going to be a problem for them.

LMS may or may not affect the ability of leisure departments and small community groups to use school facilities. Much, it seems, will be dependent on the stance adopted by governors and headteachers. More fundamental is the possible impact of the national curriculum allied to LMS on the physical education and sporting programmes which schools will be able to provide. It is possible to take a profoundly depressing view of their likely long-term consequences — and more than one of those whom we interviewed did so. At its worst, a possible future was seen to develop along the following lines which is a compilation of views expressed by officers and the elected member who was chairman of the Council's leisure committee.

Underfunding in the schools remains the major problem for governors and headteachers. Experienced staff are too expensive to retain without additional substantial income. Schools increasingly look to maximize their income from alternative sources. For those schools in well-heeled districts, parents are the obvious and effective recourse but in poorer districts their ability to top up budgets are negligible. Those schools are forced into increasing their letting charges for their premises so that groups who had traditionally used them at little or no cost find themselves excluded because of their inability to pay.

The National Curriculum, with its associated testing system — the results of which have, by law, to be published as a guide to parents in choosing a school for their children — makes it imperative that schools are seen to be 'efficient' within the terms laid down by the Education Reform Act, 1988. Schools have to make hard choices between retaining, say, a mathematics teacher and a physical education teacher. The former is crucial to the perceived success of the school and requires relatively modest capital resources for him or her to work effectively. The latter consumes huge resources by comparison and the results of his or her work count for little. The choice is made and physical education in the school is restricted to the minimum required by law. Pupils who wish to take part in organized sport are expected to join local clubs.

Increasing pressures on teachers to produce 'good results' in their major teaching subject, allied to existing contractual arrangements which specify the number of hours that can be required of them, ensure that fewer and fewer are prepared to devote evenings and weekends to promoting sports and other forms of physical recreation.

The option of joining clubs of various kinds is most likely to be taken by pupils whose parents can readily afford the expense involved and whose cultural imperatives make the expense seem worthwhile. Moreover, as Spink (1988) convincingly argues:

> Leisure facilities within inner cities are thus subject to the joint pressures of urban development processes which maintain relatively high rents and land values despite an atmosphere of cumulative decline and a resident local population impoverished and disadvantaged. Commercial viability is thus rendered marginal or impossible and only a limited range of facilities can persist in such a climate.

From this he then suggests that most leisure facilities will tend to migrate to lower-priced land in suburbia and beyond. The impact of this on the inner-city residents, of whom ethnic minority communities form a disproportionate part, will effectively be to deny them access.

One elected member was very clear on his perception of the future.

> I think there is a worse animal than CCT and that's LMS. I can't put my finger on it really, but at governor's meetings, with the tight budgets the schools have got, you can see how certain governors are thinking — inquiring about prices; how much is the hall worth to be let out at night? the fields etc? I'm quite sure with some of the mixed schools we've got with swimming pools in, the governors are thinking how to get money out of them. The capitation, as you know has been decreased year by year and they've got to work within that budget. Some of the parent governors — and you can't blame them — are thinking 'We've got our children to be educated. Now if we can have the sports field or the baths or the sports hall let, and get the money . . .', and although it's depriving those [ethnic minority] children, they'll do that to raise money to educate their children.

> Take for example a Headmaster who may think, 'Well, I could do with a French teacher, but I've only so much in my budget.' Now if he could raise money with his sports hall or his playing fields, he would raise the money to afford his French teacher. Or just to keep the staff he's got. Because with the budgets being cut, certain teacher posts will have to go. And rather than let those posts go, obviously he'll try to raise money to keep those teachers in post.

> And I think we'll see it happen in one or two years. It won't be ten years. That's my fear. It is only a fear yet, but it's my opinion.

To summarize this worst-case future from the perspective of ethnic minority groups, we have a virtual disappearance of physical education from the school curriculum together with school facilities being priced out of reach for use on a community basis. Fewer and fewer teachers are prepared to give up time out-of-hours — and, in any case, it is well established that Asian girls are unlikely to be allowed, or willing, to stay on after school. Finally, over time, facilities are re-located out of reach in suburbia. The clubs, which their middle-class white peers can join, are not accessible to Muslims of either sex if, as is usually the case, there is a bar on the premises and are anyway out of the question for young women.

More generally on the subject of schools, although it was not within our research objectives or our resources to explore current practices in any detail, we were concerned to pick up hints that there was, at best, a patchy recognition of the needs of children from ethnic minorities. Local education authorities were, of all the arms of local government, the best equipped with policies covering the various forms of equal opportunities in education, and schools were under con-siderable pressure to conform with those policies. Some LEAs made it a require-ment that schools wrote their own policy documents which interpreted those of the authority in the light of their own circumstances. Others admitted that they made no specific demands on their schools to meet the needs of ethnic minority pupils in PE and games. We quote from an interview with an Action Sport officer — a young Asian woman — to illustrate the kind of worries that we have.

Q Do you think that the children, particularly the girls, growing up through the schools now, will, like you, find it increasingly easier to take part in sports?

A They find it easier if they are working with someone like me, so they've got a role model to follow. But most of them have dropped out. When I went round the schools they said they'll only do PE to about the third year then after that they just drop out — they don't want to know about sport at all. And it's probably not the children: it's the parents. When there are mixed sessions the parents don't like that.

Q The schools don't run single-sex sessions?

A Not all of them, no. Some of the schools don't want to admit it's a problem. I've spoken to some of the girls, and I've asked them, 'Do you like doing PE?' Oh yes, they like doing PE but the time they don't like it is when they've got a mixed session. 'We like single-sex sessions but the teachers won't allow it.'

Q I find that interesting because a lot of LEAs and schools have developed policies about single-sex PE and games.

A I would have thought there would be more now. When I was at school, we used to have single PE lessons and I would have expected more. I was quite surprised when I went round schools to find that there were very few schools that did have single-sex sessions. Most of them were mixed.

Q What do the girls do when they aren't doing PE?

A Perhaps just sit there. I don't know. When they get to the third year they have options so they just don't choose PE. They choose some other option. When I was at school it was compulsory but I don't think it is now . . . I remember at one school and the teacher there was very concerned about girls not taking sports and she said that out of the whole fifth year, there was only one Asian girl that took sports. She said that some of them had been really good but once they got to the fourth year they just stopped.

On the issue of single-sex PE there seems a modest difference of opinion between the Equal Opportunities Commission and the Commission for Racial Equality. The former does not, in general, consider that it is in the interests of the majority of girls to be required to have single-sex PE classes if, in fact, they would rather have mixed-sex lessons. The latter takes the view that schools should take account of the ethnic origin of its pupils when constructing their timetables and, in particular, should have regard to the preference by many South Asian girls (and their parents) for single-sex activities. In an ideal world it would be possible for schools to accommodate both positions and enable female pupils to choose either single- or mixed-sex activities. For most schools, such a solution might well not be an option. Our own view is that schools need to be aware of the reality of the problem for South Asian girls and should, in consultation with parents, adopt policies and practices which allow, as far as possible, elements of choice. When provision for choice cannot be made, the balance of need tilts firmly in favour of single-sex provision.

The North-West Region of the Sports Council in Fact File No 1 (1990) records that, in spite of hopes that the National Curriculum and LMS would encourage the achievement of the common good, experience to date had not justified the optimism. 'The prospects for 1993 and the onset of LMS throughout the region are potentially very disturbing unless recreationalists influence decisions, provide alternative solutions and ensure that schools are directed to deliver the social policies of the authority.' We would applaud the vigorous response to the uncertainties that change brings with it, and the perception of its authors that change can be managed to produce desired ends. We would, however, add that the magnitude of the job should not be under-estimated. Whilst the particular needs of ethnic minorities are not specifically referred to, its references to the need to 'encourage schools to widen community use based on socially just policies and not simply the ability to pay' are potentially beneficial to them.

What does perturb us, however, is an underlying assumption that schools, for curricular and financial reasons may be constrained to make a smaller contribution to physical education, sport and recreation than they have done in the past and that other organizations — in their own interests as well as those of the community at large — should actively involve themselves in the work of schools. Our concern arises from what we perceive as the clash of cultures. Schools are educational institutions, concerned with the development of the individual. As another publication by the Sports Council (Education Reform Fact Sheet for Local Authority Departments) observes, 'It is important to understand that physical education is not the same as sport. Traditionally, a number of sports have looked to schools to produce their future star performers.' The difference in approach between schools and sports clubs may well create sharp dilemmas for schools as they seek to maintain a viable programme in partnership with sports clubs with fundamentally different priorities.

For pupils of South Asian origin the situation looks particularly bleak. Parents and children tend to have an instrumental approach to education. They see it as an avenue to economic and social advancement and make their educational decisions based on benefit to their projected careers. Interview evidence suggests that many parents are unconvinced that sport and physical education is of equal importance to the more academic subjects within the curriculum. They accept that their children do it because it is part of the school process. If prime responsibility for sports and games becomes effectively devolved away from education and the schools to local sports clubs, with the activities taking place out of school hours, many students in schools will be effectively debarred from participation.

The Education Reform Act and the devolution of responsibilities to schools through LMS will make it increasingly difficult to monitor schools' provision in the future. Even if monitoring were undertaken, the powers given to governors and headteachers makes it seem unlikely that much could be done, other than exhortation.

However, we note that the Major administration has located the Minister for Sport in the Department of Education and Science (DES, now DFE), rather than in Environment. This might have a significant and beneficial impact on the relationship between the Sports Council and the education service.

We repeat, it was not part of our brief and we lacked the resources to investigate the current and evolving situation in schools in proper detail. We would suggest that the ways that schools respond to the combined pressures of LMS and the National Curriculum in their physical education provision may disadvantage all pupils but that those of South Asian origin are particularly vulnerable.

The Youth and Community Service

It was during the course of the study that we became increasingly aware of the work done by the Youth and Community Service with ethnic minority groups — not least in encouraging participation in sports and outdoor activities generally.

We were able to record interviews with members of the Service from most of the authorities in Greater Manchester and were much impressed, not only by what they were doing with modest resources but also — and in our view, very importantly — by the strategies they adopted to achieve their ends. The Youth and Community Service is normally, indeed almost exclusively, located within the local authority structure as part of the Education Service. Its primary concern is the social, moral and intellectual development of young people, the majority of whom are likely to be youngsters who have left school at sixteen. In most authorities, the priority clients within that group are seen as the disadvantaged and deprived, which inevitably includes young people from the ethnic minorities.

It is worth noting that the Youth and Community Service is the only statutory organization with responsibility for young people at the point of transition from school to adult life. Although it is normally part of the education department, its funding is perhaps the least secure of any of that department's activities. The departments inevitably give priority to the schools for which they have a statutory responsibility, followed by their further education service with youth and community coming last. This leads to chronic under-funding as the rule. We found that many officers were oppressed by a sense of being undervalued in their work which was only made tolerable by the belief they had in its value to the young people they worked for.

Sport and outdoor recreation plays an important part in their work. Their objectives are not the achievement of sporting excellence. A typical comment was:

> We aren't set up for standards of excellence. If we have a youngster who is good at sport and has the potential, then we move them on to an area where [he will be trained by] people who are more skilled than we are.

But that didn't prevent a later statement, made with some pride and pleasure:

> . . . but the lads themselves that we're with, they're just the same as any. The football team, the cricket team, they're in there to win, and, in fact, we've got a football team down there and they're winning everything they play for.

The Service (in common no doubt with every other arm of local government) saw itself as chronically under-funded for all its activities. Common observation during the course of our visits suggested that, with the exception of one authority, they were. The one exception was fortunate in having a very effective officer at its head who was, in turn, lucky to have a council which fully supported his efforts. He was able to gesture towards a storeroom and tell us that there was '£250,000 worth of gear there.' The benefits to his work and the youngsters were obvious.

> It doesn't matter what state [a young person's] in when they come here. When he goes out to the bus he'll be properly equipped for whatever activity he's going to take on. Now that's part of positive discrimination. We often find that Asian young people have a reputation for not wanting to be involved in outdoor education. Our experience is totally to the contrary. Provided you equip them properly and they've got confidence in the staff, they're as keen and eager to climb mountains as anybody . . . And some of the Asian women too, given the opportunity and the confidence — and that comes from believing that *they are* properly

equipped, that they are 'safe' if you like, and that we will take care of them.

We would repeat, however, that this was an exceptional case and served only to throw into sharp relief the plight of departments in other authorities.

We asked about actual or possible connexions with and help from the Sports Council. The problem for the Service lay, as much as anything, with the structure of local government. As one Youth and Community officer put it — and he could well have been speaking for all but one of those we interviewed —

> . . . there seems to be some understanding, engendered by whom I'm not quite sure, that the Sports Council shall relate to leisure services. And if you look at the local authority lead officer with the Sports Council, he is located in the Recreational Services Department. He owes me no allegiance so he doesn't send me anything . . .

We also inquired about the relationships between Youth and Community Services and leisure service departments. Again, with one exception, it seemed that they were seen as separate — and often competing — organizations within the local authority structure. At the managerial/structural level it seemed to us that there was, at best, a cold war situation. When we put this perception to officers in the Youth and Community Service there was general agreement that it was correct except, as one of them put it, 'when things got difficult and a shooting war broke out.' In terms of service delivery to ethnic minority groups, the results of this were seen as harmful and a sad waste of resources:

> I think it's also important that the consequential effects of this sort of demarcation is that Action Sport is not with me. It's with leisure services. We are actually doing a parallel programme and we're not getting funding for it because leisure services [officially] deliver it — for whatever reason. There are pretty good informal networking arrangements but we're never permitted to know how much is being invested in that programme, what the target age range is . . . We become aware that they are operating in one of our patches and they use bits and pieces of our resources that they don't have, and we are not consulted about joint management or priority areas as we see them.

> It's a bit ironic when the new theme is 'progress through partnership' as seen by the Sports Council — of drawing together agencies to improve facilities for all classes of the community, for Sport for All.

It may be that its strategy for meeting local needs is the result of necessity. Be that as it may, it is none the less impressive. In its essence lay the proposition that the Youth and Community Service workers enabled, empowered, communities to achieve their own ends. It manages this by deeply involving itself in the

73

communities, helping them to identify what they want, helping them to do what they want, and making them responsible for the project, whatever it might be when it is completed. An example would be the development of an all-weather pitch at a junior school in a social priority area.

> What we're talking about isn't a plush, sports-centre-type provision, but it's something that is very locally managed, which is managed deliberately on a shoe-string but is responsive to the needs of the community. It isn't about £150,000 worth of bricks and mortar: it's about play-space ... It's about ownership, about identification ... As the young people have to manage it, they have to learn ... So, again, with the management of their pitch, they're going to learn the hard way that there's no easy way to manage recreational facilities and there's no easy way to set priorities. Doing that, we're hoping that they will also begin to learn the very real problems of managing ... and recognizing the value of it, adopting it and protecting it ...

> You see, the difference between that sort of facility and a recreational [department] facility. They go in and pay their fee and they might have a series of coaching opportunities — and that's it! Whereas, if they go into a situation within the Youth and Community ethos they not only have the opportunity of doing the coaching course; people there are genuinely interested in the well-being of that young person. That is not meant to be disrespectful of colleagues in recreational departments ...

Located, as they are, within departments of education, the Youth and Community officers are very much affected by the education ethos. We have commented earlier on the general failure of local authorities to consider positive action in the context of service delivery whilst making much of their intentions over employment. Our previous work in studying and researching the education service (and indeed the work of many others in the field) has revealed that — with whatever success in practice — the concern of Departments of Education has been, first and foremost, with service delivery. This concern was reflected in the attitudes of the Youth and Community Service. The focus of their attention was the young people and this shone through every interview we were able to conduct. It was *through* the various activities — and these were at least as varied and challenging as those afforded through the leisure department — that the Youth and Community Service sought to achieve its objectives. They were not the ends in themselves.

We wish to stress this difference and make no apology for dwelling on it. Whereas the general concern and primary focus of leisure departments was with the promotion of sports and outdoor pursuits — consider, for a moment, the significance of the titles employed within the leisure departments: Sports Development Officer, Action Sport Officer — the focus of the Youth and Community Service was the development of the young people that were their clients. This difference of approach between the two types of department made for a very different relationship between them and the people with whom they were working or wished to work.

It was this, we believe, that goes far to account for the relative success of the Youth and Community Service in recruiting voluntary workers from ethnic minority communities. One officer with a foot in both camps said:

> It would be interesting to see if there's any opportunity for young people [from ethnic minority groups] to be involved in decision-making in the leisure services. To date that's not been seen. And looking at it from the Sports Council's point of view, there are very few up and coming . . . When I go to committee meetings it's very rare to see a colleague from an ethnic minority group there.

There was consistent evidence of commitment to meeting the needs of ethnic minorities in the service and a willingness to go to considerable lengths to do so. Thus:

> We've set up a basic training course . . . and we've now got five Asian ladies who are coming on. We've had to completely reorganize the course so that it's done during the daytime and women only. A man who would normally be the trainer has been replaced by me so that they will be able to attend. We have no doubt that we'll never get these Asian women to work in other than Asian groups but we're committed to encouraging them to come along. We left 25 per cent of the places for ethnic minorities and we've had five women apply. Now whether they actually turn up on the first day is another matter, but we've made these special arrangements so they won't have to associate with men and they won't have to go out in the evening. And at the end of it they'll be qualified youth and community workers.

From another authority which had been successful in attracting external funding for its Youth and Community Work Apprenticeship we heard:

> . . . we are required as a consequence of having bid for that resource to recruit and train ten young people between the ages of 18–25 from within the borough boundary . . . and over that three-year period to deliver the equivalent of a professional qualification in youth and community work. *Six* of those ten are drawn from the Asian community, three young women and three young men. It was quite a deliberate decision.
>
> Q Did you have any difficulty in recruiting them?
> A We worked very hard in order to make sure. We put the word out on the grapevine, we held consultation meetings, we did everything we possibly could do to make sure that we reached all ethnic minority

groups. We had, in the end, eighty applications for the ten places of which twenty-five were from the Asian community . . .

. . . Out of the past thirteen appointments that have been made [to the Service] eight have been Asian workers. What I'm trying to say is, only as and when you begin to put people out there on the street, so to speak, and within the communities to say 'We're here. What can we do for you?' In a way, no amount of translated documents are going to help. It's about the credibility within the community of what you are offering and the extent to which you are able to deliver.

As well as operating through positive recruitment campaigns like that, the Youth and Community Service benefits from its long-established practices. We recall a conversation with a young Asian where he was working in a community centre in the middle of a very depressed area. We asked him how he came to be doing his present job.

When this place first opened it was a school and it switched to being a youth centre. When we started about '73–74, my [elder] brother used to come to this place. And my brother started working here and I came with him. And I knew most of the lads here anyway and about '85 Tony asked me to come here, and it just happened, like that.

Shortly after that conversation he was due to embark on a two-year full-time course for a qualification in youth and community work.

There were other potential benefits from being closely associated with the work of the education service. As one head of department put it,

I think we have a real problem. In a sense we have something of a credibility problem with the Asian communities. Because we're seen — because of discos and juke boxes and things we have in our youth clubs — we have an image problem of Western decadence. Now it means we have a task to perform to persuade that Asian population to understand that we're part of the education service. Because being part of the education service gives us some of the legitimacy of the school side.

The leisure department has absolutely no chance because that's not seen as Western decadence, it's seen as everybody having an equal opportunity provided they can afford the cost of admission, and therefore it's not a controlled situation in Muslim terms. We are half-way house if you like, which is not fully exploited. Now in some senses, one of our prime tasks may be to get this across: that most of the workers in the Youth and Community Service are teachers. It's the educational thing. The Muslim community actually do recognize education.

For those working in the Youth and Community Service, LMS and the National Curriculum were seen as a direct challenge to prepare to meet the losses which many foresaw.

> The market economy in schooling is going to put headteachers in the position where they have to consider, endlessly, their academic credibility. Because academic credibility is allied to numbers going through the school gate. Numbers through the school gate in a falling [birthrate] situation is survival, so anything that doesn't add to that academic credibility is perhaps low priority . . .

> I don't think that in school they can offer much at all [in the way of sport] within a double lesson a week. How can you follow anything through? This seems to have potentially serious consequences for precisely the youngsters we are concerned with. It also has an effect on the general fitness of the country. If this department doesn't offer an opportunity for them to participate in an active lifestyle either before, or at the point of leaving school, it doesn't augur well for when they leave . . .

We have written about the benefits — as we perceived them — of working within the education service from the point of view of service delivery and relationships with their clients. We only referred in passing to the disadvantages. One of these is the competition for resources which is made the more acute at a time when local authorities are increasingly constrained. This made for a great sense of professional frustration and not a little cynicism. One head of a Youth and Community Division spoke of the way attitudes to the service changed after there had been a serious racial incident.

> . . . They [the authority] are skint at the moment — more than they usually are . . . And youth work is not the prime area to receive support. People don't understand the work you are trying to do. They'll say 'Get those kids off the street. They want a youth club — *not near our house!*' I mean, in Nonesuch the youth club is totally ignored until such time as incidents like that occur and then it's 'What's the youth club doing? Why isn't the Youth Service responding to this?' And we all get called to meetings where we all sit around and discuss what we should be doing, and why aren't we doing it, and it boils down to cash at the end of the day. And we object most strongly to the fact that we were given a small amount of money. You build up people's expectations and then the money's taken away from you. And really the heat has gone out of the situation and it's all calmed down. We haven't had an [incident] lately.

> I've been here fifteen years. One does tend to get a little cynical. We get extremely frustrated by it. We need money for long-term projects.

We don't want £4,000 to do something till 1 January and then there's nothing left.

When something like this happens . . . They go through these exercises and when something happens they think 'Who can we stick in the firing line now? The Youth and Community Department! They're responsible for that.' But they may be responsible but they're like a group of soldiers with no ammunition to do anything.

We followed up this interview with a visit to the youth club set in the centre of the Asian community in which the incident occurred. It was housed in the ground floor of a free-standing building which was part of the school in whose playground it stood. It had, at one time, the use of the first floor as well but this had been reoccupied by the school because of the increasing numbers of children. A volunteer Asian youth worker told us:

. . . whereas two years before we were pleading for money and there was no response. It's got to take a major incident for you to have money. In other words, 'An [incident] a year will keep us afloat . . .'

That's the only way. That's the viewpoint they've got now. They think, 'Well, they'll let us come in for six days [a week] just after the [incident].' You know. And when things get back to normal, they think, 'Well, it's all over now.' What's it going to take. Another murder? Or perhaps just burn a few buildings. That's what would have happened during the period if we hadn't given a lot of overtime.

This objection to being seen as, and used as, fire-fighters in a social tinder-box seemed very understandable. It was made the more acute by the awareness of the need for long-term programmes if change was to be achieved. Pockets of cash that had to be used or lost and were devoted to special events were commonly spoken of and the consensus was that they often did as much harm as good. Thus:

The [education] department was asked if we would put on a [special] weekend which [Mary] was made responsible for sorting out . . . And we had 150 youngsters each day, doing sports English people didn't normally take part in. And the biggest group each day was a group of Asian lads who were absolutely tremendous. And the feeling at the end of it was 'Could we do another one?' Well, we can't because we don't have the funds to do it. It was a special, one-off opportunity.

Others were even more emphatic about the dangers of financial 'ad hocery' and pointed to the self-evident dangers of raising the hopes and expectations of young people by putting on special events which could not be followed up. As one officer said:

> We're all in this business — we hear about a pocket of money and pow! we're in there. And then expectations are raised which we cannot actually sustain and so the product is that it is worse than if we hadn't done it all! Because all we have done is disillusion a group of young people and more than that, we've disillusioned a group of committed adults.

There was a keen awareness throughout the service of the need for sustained, long-term commitment if barriers to access were to be broken down and ethnic minority youngsters were to have real equality of opportunity. This may, in part have been because there seemed to be a much greater sense of the reality of racism in society at large and the social injustice that flowed from it than we found in other local authority departments.

As we noted above, in our discussions with officers in leisure departments there seemed almost a reluctance to recognize that racism might exist within the the larger community. Youth and Community officers were in no doubt about it.

> **Q** Do you think there is much racism in [the area]?
> **A** I think there is, yes. There's a lot of lip-service paid to the fact that there isn't, but there is. There's a lot of resentment about the fact that [minority] groups will apply to have a community centre built for them and the Council will seriously think about spending about £150,000. And then you get 'Well, [a white district] can't have a community centre!' And then nobody gets it because there's no money.

Allied to this greater awareness in the Youth and Community Service was a higher level of understanding about the nature of racism and the ways it impinged on the different minority communities. There was also a greater knowledge about the ethnic minority communities in their areas, their cultures and the ways in which cultural differences affected their ability or willingness to engage at any level with the white majority.

Information Gathering

A question taken up with many senior officers in local authorities was their sources of information on which to base their programmes for ethnic minority groups. How did they find out what was wanted or needed? One was able to say:

> We do have a number of staff working out in the area whose role is basically to be involved with Action Sport-type initiatives . . . Their brief is to go out and find what the community wants and what they feel about what we are trying to achieve . . .

The point I was trying to make is that, yes, we do get some non-systematic feedback, but the information that those staff get isn't necessarily recorded . . . They retain it but, you know, we don't have any recording system. And we don't necessarily have any mechanism for relating what we do, what our policies are, to the information that they have which they keep to themselves . . .

Actually, operational staff have day-to-day contact with visitors to the facilities, feedback in the course of normal conversations: not recorded, only acted on at local level at the discretion of the officer in charge.

Another authority was in the process of restructuring its service delivery over a wide range of its services (including leisure) which directly affected the public and saw the potential for great advantages resulting therefrom.

Each neighbourhood centre will be run by a management committee which will have local residents on it. The whole idea behind it is basically decentralization of services which will help us to become more responsive to local community needs and also to integrate the services, so that we can work together with community education, social services . . .

We have this corporate strategy document which outlines the priority areas . . . and the priority groups [women, ethnic minorities, disabled and unemployed] are very important in times of limited resources as far as leisure services are concerned . . . We see that we want to channel our resources into the main priority groups as far as possible.

Elsewhere we had much less positive responses. As one second-tier officer bluntly said:

If I could give you an answer to that I wouldn't be doing this job: I'd be much higher up the tree. I think the determination of community needs is something that has taxed the minds of practitioners and academics for years.

On visiting another leisure department we were encouraged to notice a map on the wall with the location of all known ethnic minority community centres within the authority marked in red. We were told that, some four years previously, a programme of visits had been set up with the view to maintaining continuous consultation with the minority groups. At that time there had been some fourteen, including YTS (Youth Training Scheme) trainees in the section. At the time of our visit there were two (plus two YTS trainees) in post. Consultation had ceased two years ago. There was clearly no prospect of its being revived. At the time of the interview we failed to establish whether this was the result of economies by the authority or changes in its priority in leisure provision. Whatever the reason, a strategy which we believe to be highly promising had necessarily been discarded.

In the main there was an assumption that Sports Development Officers and particularly those in Action Sport were in contact with the grassroots, with the community, and were picking up the vibrations. Having done that, it was for them to act effectively on the basis of their personal insights, related (where they existed) to the policies of the department and the council. In some cases there seemed to be some justification for this and we explore the reasons for that success below. We have to say, however, that, in our view, this approach seemed to place far too much responsibility on relatively junior officers who were not necessarily equipped with the skills, personal experience or resources to do the job.

Their difficulties were clearly compounded by the frequent lack of a departmental policy to serve as a framework for their activities. Moreover, the *de facto* policy of some seemed to be to maximize participation and, hence, income to the council so that they might well find themselves struggling against the tide of events rather than supported by the department as a whole. (One Sports Development Officer confided in us that there had been a time in the recent past, before a change at head of department level, when he and his colleagues (all male) had to meet in the men's lavatory whenever they wanted to discuss plans for anything related to positive action.)

As we noted above, there was little in the way of systematic monitoring of use of facilities. The one council that did conduct a survey on the use of its facilities had no ethnic question. Only one of the ten authorities we surveyed had any hard data *at all* on the use made of its leisure facilities by its ethnic minority population and that had been collected in the course of a survey conducted, not by the leisure department but by another department essentially for other purposes.

Monitoring service delivery and take-up by identified groups within the total community is difficult, time-consuming and has resource implications. Local authorities have seldom in the past seen any necessity for it. Services were provided either because they were under a legal obligation (housing and education, for instance) with clients whose rights to the service were established by statute, or were part of what was seen as their general social and cultural obligation, such as museums, art galleries, parks and gardens and recreational facilities. The level of provision in this type of service was established on a pragmatic basis but the unspoken assumptions were that provision should be adequate to meet the needs of all those who wished to use them and that all who wished to use them would, and could, do so. It is only recently and in some authorities that these assumptions have come to be questioned. It might be accounted a misfortune that the issue of positive action in service provision has arisen when no data exists on which to base action and when resources cannot be found to generate the data, even when there is a will to do so.

We found the fact that no effective systems existed to collect information particularly worrying in the context of this study since we were frequently told by officers of the Sports Council that they looked to local authorities for information on which to base policies and practices.

Action Sport

Many of our inquiries about the ways in which leisure departments were tackling the needs of ethnic minorities were met with the response that it was through the work of Action Sport personnel. The degree of priority they gave to this aspect of their work varied from one authority to another. In general terms, those authorities with the largest numbers of people from minority groups gave higher priority to it than those with fewer but this was not always the case.

In establishing target groups, the leisure departments were clearly influenced by the Sports Council's own target groups — young people, women and the 45–59 year-olds and within those broad groups, disabled people, the unemployed and ethnic minorities. The actual priority given to any particular group seemed to be a function of the perceived level of need within the authority's population, the inclinations of the officers and to some degree, the preferences of the ruling party at local level.

We would pay tribute to the efforts of many of the Action Sports officers whom we were able to interview. As might be deduced from earlier parts of this section, we felt that they were faced with awesomely difficult tasks. Their youth, their junior position within their organizations, the policy vacuum in which most of them had to operate and, in a number of cases at least, their insecurity of tenure, all made for operational difficulties which must have been very difficult for them to overcome.

It was not surprising that some of the most successful Action Sport officers were from the same minority groups as those they were trying to serve. This was particularly true when the target groups were Muslims from Bangladesh or Pakistan and especially the women in those groups. At the risk of appearing to grossly over-simplify matters, a central issue that emerged in interviews was that of trust. The community — and in this context we mean the men of the community — have to trust the officer with their wives and daughters, and this trust has to be earned. One very successful officer, herself a remarkable young Muslim woman, admitted that she was very fortunate in having unusually liberal-minded parents.

> I mean, my parents weren't as liberal a few years back as they are today . . . But that's because I had to build up that trust. I had to make sure that my parents could trust me . . . There are lots of girls who say 'Oh, you're so lucky; your parents don't mind. You can go away for a weekend and stay with the group and your parents don't mind.' But I've had to build that trust.

During the course of an interview we explored the secret of her success as she saw it. We suggested that it could not be achieved in the course of a few months but must be the result of a much greater investment of time.

> No you can't [manage it in a few months]. No way! I used to work as a part-time worker, a voluntary youth worker at [a community centre]. Because I had no job at the time, and I really enjoyed doing that sort of work.

> When I was a voluntary worker it wasn't really to do with sports. It was just something to get women out of the house. They used to come along and do things like sewing and reading in the mother tongue and similar things. And they got to know me there.

> And then Action Sport . . . wanted an Asian woman to do sports with them. And they wanted it for a trial period of six months. And it [news that someone was needed] happened to come to me; so they interviewed me. I decided I would take it on, just to see what I could do.

At the time of the interview she had been working for her ethnic minority community in one capacity or another for nearly five years and had been known by many within it for most of her life. The consequence was that she had earned the trust of husbands and fathers in the same way that she had earned the trust of her own parents.

It was our impression (and in the absence of firm data, on which we have already commented, it could be no more than that) that the only ethnic minority officers in leisure departments were Action Sport Officers who had been appointed to encourage participation by people of the same ethnic origin. The absence of more senior ethnic minority staff within the departments with whom they could discuss their work and who would be in a position to support them is a matter for regret.

We would like to emphasize that not all Action Sport Officers were from ethnic minority groups and that many white officers were doing excellent work with ethnic minority communities in their authorities.

Many of the Action Sport Officers we spoke to had been appointed to increase participation by women and particularly South Asian women. Our summary and comments which follow relate to their experiences. We have stressed the importance they placed on winning the trust of the target group, emphasized that this must be regarded as a long-term activity and stressed the value of having officers of the same ethnic origin as the people with whom they are working.

In the course of interviews and informal conversations with Action Sport Officers it became clear that successful groups often came together originally for activities quite other than sport. Many, particularly those made up of South Asian women, started as an English as a Second Language class, or a sewing or cookery group and were introduced gradually by way of gentle keep-fit sessions. With the growth of confidence in themselves and those working with them, they were able to progress to a range of other activities. As the quotation above makes clear, there is an interest and a willingness — given the right circumstances — to take part.

Obstacles to participation included the distrust felt by many South Asian men of the social, cultural and moral norms of British society and the reluctance they felt to expose their wives and daughters to them. To this should be added the perceptions of many of the women about their own place in society and their misgivings about the propriety of what they were being asked to do. (These considerations should be read in conjunction with the relevant parts of the section on the ethnic minority communities.) At a more practical level was the need to provide transport for them to and from the activity and at minimal or no cost, since the majority had no money of their own. Flexible timing of the activities was essential so that family responsibilities would not be compromised. Afternoons were often the best time but it was a matter of negotiation on a group-by-group basis. Crèche facilities were often vital, though the detailed arrangements for these varied from group to group. Some, for example, felt that it was essential that the crèche should be run by a member of the same ethnic origin whilst others did not see this as important. Attendance was severely affected by religious festivals. Once these caused absence, the officer would normally have to make a renewed effort to persuade members to resume attendance at activities. Finally, holidays taken by the officer seemed invariably to cause the group to discontinue. The trust they had given was personalized and seemed to be nontransferable, even to one of their own members if she could be persuaded to act as leader of the group. On return, the officer would have to visit the group's members and assure them that she was back and that she wanted them to start again — even though she had explained to them that she was taking some leave and that the activity would resume on a given date.

Conclusions

Local Authorities

The local authorities which were included in our survey were at various stages in the development of their policy documents. They were often, but not invariably, influenced by their perceptions of local situations as regards their ethnic minority communities. These perceptions were seldom supported by anything more substantial than the statistics supplied by the 1981 census.

As policy documents, they were largely no more than statements of intent and often seriously flawed by the lack of clear objectives or descriptions of the processes by which the policy goals were to be realized. All placed a heavy emphasis on the need for equality in employment. Few related their responsibility for the provision of services to the needs of their ethnic minority communities.

Where, as in most cases, there was an absence of clearly defined objectives in either employment or service delivery, no monitoring systems could be put in place to measure the effectiveness of what was intended.

Leisure Departments

Leisure departments felt bound by their authorities' corporate statements of intent. Like their parent authorities, they lacked the data needed for them to act effectively. CCT and, to a lesser extent, LMS was changing their relationships with their clients in quite profound ways during the course of the study. We formed the impression that the process was forcing them to address issues that had long lain dormant and in so doing they had turned to the target group concept as established by the Sports Council as a way of ordering their priorities. Thus, ethnic minority groups may well benefit. One leisure department at least was responding positively to the challenge. What troubled us, however, was the thought that, in general, the pressures of time and events meant that they were moving from one set of practices to another without first developing policies which would properly underpin them or having the time to learn about their target groups or to establish relationships with them.

The absence of routine, systematic data collection and analysis which would make it possible to identify low participation groups was a matter for concern. Without such information it is hard to see how leisure departments can know who they are reaching. Without that knowledge, planning to reach low participation groups cannot be realistically undertaken, nor is it possible to present a case for additional funding, either within the authority or from external sources, such as the Home Office for Section 11 money.

Section 11 of the Local Government Act was the first government intervention to provide assistance to multi-racial areas. Originally such a grant was at the rate of 50 per cent of expenditure but this was later increased to 75 per cent. This grant, administered by the Home Office, has been used primarily by social services and education authorities although it was designed to cover all staff employed by local authority departments.

Far too much, in our opinion, was expected of Action Sport officers appointed with a brief to increase ethnic minority participation. All gave assurances during interviews that colleagues within the departments were helpful and supportive. We were, however, unconvinced that departments, as institutional entities, saw their work as part of its mainstream activity. Our concern was reinforced by the fact that, with few exceptions, the more senior the officer we were with, the greater the tendency to call the Action Sport officer in to discuss the specific needs of ethnic minority groups and the way that the department was responding to those needs. Work with ethnic minorities cannot be effective, is not serious, if it is seen as an optional extra to the mainstream work of the department. We see the apparent demarcation as all the more disquieting in the context of CCT.

All this weighed the more heavily in the context of our perception of the possible future patterns of leisure provision. If it is correct — that local authority provision will increasingly become the only provision to which the young and financially disadvantaged will realistically have access — it follows that:

i) Leisure departments must adopt policies and practices directed towards their real market; and,

ii) recognize that young people from ethnic minorities — particularly those of South Asian origin — form an increasing proportion of their potential clients.

Youth and Community Service

As our research shows, we were very impressed both by the Youth and Community Services' approach to their work with young people from ethnic minorities and with what they were achieving. We would emphasize that the two are intimately connected. In policy terms they were at an advantage because of their institutional location within the education departments of local authorities. Whilst local education authorities and schools — indeed the education service as a whole — still has much to learn and to put into practice over the education of young people from ethnic minorities, they are among the most advanced of all the services in their thinking, their working relationships with ethnic minorities and in their service delivery.

It was our opinion that the Youth and Community Service has much to offer the Sports Council in terms of access to ethnic minority groups both as an active partner and a model for future development.

Governing Bodies of Sport

We would not wish to place too much weight at the level of detail on the results of the postal survey on which we reported. In broad brush terms, however, the responses made it clear that most governing bodies have no policies to encourage greater participation by ethnic minority groups. Of those who responded to our inquiry, many demonstrated that they did not understand the issue. Others (though they were very much the minority) did show such an awareness and a willingness to accept that it was their responsibility, not only to encourage participation by ethnic minorities as players but also as managers.

Notes

1 Under Section 1 of the Race Relations Act (1976), indirect discrimination occurs when: 'A person discriminates against another in any circumstances relevant for the

purposes of any provision of this act if . . . b) he applies to that other a requirement or condition which he applies or would apply equally to persons not of the same racial group as that other but i) which is such that the proportion of persons of the same racial group as that other who can comply with it is considerably smaller than the proportion of persons not of that racial group who can comply with it; and ii) which he cannot show to be justifiable irrespective of the colour, race, nationality or ethnic origins of the persons to whom it is applied; and iii) which is to the detriment of that other because he cannot comply with it.

Chapter 5

Sport and Life

Introduction

It was recognized from the outset that this research might present difficulties because of the sensitivities associated with issues of race and ethnicity. Some of the difficulties proved to be more serious than anticipated. The timing of the project coincided with the publication of Salman Rushdie's *Satanic Verses*; at the same time there were formal applications to the Secretary of State for Education for the creation of separate schools for Muslims which he was to reject; and proposals for the National Curriculum in schools were perceived in some quarters as being potentially alienating. While there is no direct evidence that any of these affected the research, they did nothing to make the overall climate more conducive to the collection of data from minority ethnic groups.

Access to communities was attempted in the first place through the cooperation of community organizations — sometimes successfully, sometimes not — in order to lessen the chances of alienation, but this may have led to the samples becoming more 'opportunistic' or 'available' than truly representative. While a balance was kept as far as possible between the genders, age groups, types of housing, and employment, it was not possible to say that each group was a fully representative sample of the community from which it was taken. This is because insufficient data existed to define the communities, and also because information could only be collected from those people who were prepared to give it. There were inevitably some variations on the ways which the field workers had to employ in order to gain access to respondents which may have led to undetected biases. Such difficulties may be inherent in all social science research, and should be borne in mind when any attempt is made to extrapolate the results of this research to other situations and communities. Despite these constraints, the similarities between the groups in terms of age, gender, employment and housing were more marked than were the differences, and the consistency of the data made it possible for us to believe that we were comparing like with like.

In designing the study, attempts were made to locate any findings with regard to sporting and recreational activities firmly in their context. In chapter 4 we surveyed some of the institutional contexts in which physical activities take place. In this section we set out our findings from the survey of respondents from ethnic minorities in Greater Manchester, supplemented by material from recorded interviews with members of the communities.

Table 4: Ethnic Origin by Age and by Gender

Age Band		Bang	Afr	Caribb	Chin	EAA	Indian	Pak	W/Brit	Other
16–20	(M)	29	10	12	30	5	33	23	33	5
	(M%)*	47.5	40.1	27.3	42.3	31.3	34.0	43.4	34.4	
	(F)	26	9	26	50	4	20	39	38	2
	(F%)	57.8	42.9	33.8	70.4	50.0	35.7	38.6	34.5	
21–25	(M)	18	8	13	23	2	36	14	34	3
	(M%)	29.5	32.0	29.5	32.4	12.5	37.1	26.4	35.4	
	(F)	11	9	27	14	–	26	19	39	2
	(F%)	24.4	42.9	35.1	19.7	–	46.4	18.8	35.5	
26+	(M)	13	6	18	11	9	23	13	27	1
	(M%)	21.3	24.0	40.9	15.5	56.3	23.7	24.5	28.1	
	(F)	7	3	22	5	1	9	35	29	3
	(F%)	15.6	14.3	28.6	7.0	12.5	16.1	34.7	26.4	

* The percentages give the proportions of males or females in each age band by their ethnic origin.

The interview material frequently consists of quite lengthy passages which throw light on a number of issues. Obviously they are concerned in one way or another with some aspect of sport. They were also intended to show how people's social and cultural heritages affect the totality of their lives. Ethnic minority groups face an array of challenges from the majority. They take many forms. Most obviously there is racism in all its forms, direct and indirect, intentional and unintentional, personal and institutional. However, and it cannot be said too loudly, racism is a problem which afflicts the majority, even though it is the minorities which suffer from it. Many of the interviews showed how aspects of Western European culture which are highly prized — personal freedom, personal responsibility, the relationship between parents and children, feminism, current notions of sexual morality, to name but a few — were regarded with distrust by people from ethnic minorities. They also show how these issues affect their willingness and ability to take part in many of the activities open to the white majority.

Although the interviews were recorded with people living in Greater Manchester, we are confident that many of the misgivings expressed by people from ethnic minority groups would be found in similar people living anywhere in Britain.

The Sample

Table 4 sets out the sample we were able to take and divides it into the respondents' self-assessed ethnic origins, ages and genders. As may be seen, the gender balance by ethnic origin and within the age bands (which are those used throughout the section wherever we suspect that age might be a factor to be reckoned with) was maintained within acceptable limits. It may also be noted that the proportions within each age band accorded well with the known demographic patterns. Thus, there was a preponderance of young Bangladeshis, Indians and Pakistanis,

Table 5: Place of Birth by Ethnic Origin

Ethnic Origin	Bang	Afr	Carib	Chin	EAA	Ind	Pak	UK	Other
Bangladeshi	78	–	–	–	–	–	1	26	1
%	73.6	–	–	–	–	–	0.9	24.5	0.9
African	–	14	–	–	–	–	–	27	5
%	–	30.4	–	–	–	–	–	58.7	10.8
Caribbean	–	2	26	–	–	–	–	93	–
%	–	1.7	21.5	–	–	–	–	76.9	–
Chinese	–	–	–	48	–	–	–	62	32
%	–	–	–	33.8	–	–	–	43.7	30.0
EAA	–	2	–	–	14	–	–	6	2
%	–	8.3	–	–	58.3	–	–	25.0	8.3
Indian	–	17	–	–	10	28	–	90	8
%	–	11.1	–	–	6.5	18.3	–	58.8	5.3
Pakistani	–	–	1	–	–	7	77	68	1
%	–	–	0.6	–	–	4.5	50.0	44.2	0.2
W/British	–	1	–	1	–	1	–	193	10
%	–	0.5	–	0.5	–	0.5	–	93.7	5.0

whilst respondents from the Caribbean, East African Asian and white British communities reflected the more even balance of mature communities. We were less successful with the Chinese respondents, who were markedly skewed towards the younger end of the age range under investigation, and it is clear that this contributes towards their high participation rates which become evident later.

Table 5 gives their places of birth by ethnic origin. Again, the responses are very much in line with what would be expected from census data. Bangladeshis, as the most recent settlers, show the greatest proportion of respondents who were born in their homeland (73.6 per cent) followed by Pakistanis (50 per cent) whose major settlement phase immediately preceded theirs and has now effectively ended. Of the other ethnic minority groups, the Caribbean (76.9 per cent) and Indian (58.8 per cent) communities have the largest proportions of British-born respondents.

Table 6 gives the religious beliefs of the sample by ethnic origin. As might be expected from the earlier outline description of these two communities, 96.8 per cent of Pakistani and 92.5 per cent of Bangladeshi respondents gave Islam as their belief. The Indian community was more complex. Just over a third (35.3 per cent) were Hindus, one-third were Sikhs, 12.5 per cent said they were agnostic or atheist and the remainder were Muslims or followed some other religion. The African and West Indian communities were roughly comparable: some two-thirds of both professed Christianity, with the most prominent other group in the two communities being agnostic or atheists. The small sample of East African Asians was equally divided between Islam and Hinduism. Somewhat more than half (53.4 per cent) of the white British community were Christian and virtually the rest were atheists or agnostics (39.3 per cent). Buddhism, Rastafarianism, Taoism and other religions were scarcely significant across the whole sample. Of the unbelievers, the Chinese community provided the greatest proportion (59.9 per cent) followed by the white British (39.3 per cent) and the West Indians (28.9

Table 6: Religious Belief by Ethnic Origin

Religion	Bang	Afr	Carib	Chin	EAA	Ind	Pak	W/Brit	Other
Buddhism	–	–	–	11	–	–	–	3	2
%	–	–	–	7.7	–	–	–	1.5	
Christianity	–	28	81	45	–	3	–	110	5
%	–	60.9	66.9	31.7	–	2.0	–	53.4	
Hinduism	7	–	–	–	10	54	–	–	–
%	6.6	–	–	–	41.7	35.3	–	–	–
Islam	98	5	1	–	11	24	149	7	2
%	92.5	10.9	0.8	–	45.8	15.7	96.8	3.4	
Rasta	–	1	1	–	–	–	–	1	–
%	–	2.2	0.8	–	–	–	–	0.5	
Sikhism	–	–	–	–	–	51	–	–	–
%	–	–	–	–	–	33.3	–	–	–
Taoism	–	–	–	1	–	–	–	–	–
%	–	–	–	0.7	–	–	–	–	–
Other	–	4	3	–	–	1	1	4	2
%	–	8.7	2.5	–	–	0.7	0.6	1.9	
Agnostic/Atheist	1	8	35	85	3	20	4	81	5
%	0.9	17.4	28.9	59.9	12.5	13.1	2.6	39.3	

per cent). We found none of these data surprising except for the extent to which they accorded with the generally descriptive accounts given in the section on the ethnic minority communities.

We were interested in the impact of ethnicity (if any) on the way that friendships developed and the way they were perceived by our respondents. Some problems emerged with this part of the survey, unfortunately after the pilot. The question asked respondents to say how many of their close friends were of the same or other ethnic origins. We had not recognized the problem that the word 'close' might pose, particularly to the younger end of the sample. Too late, we came to realize that the concept of 'close friends' was one that many — across the ethnic boundaries — found difficult to handle. Particularly the young people insisted that friends were friends and refused to distinguish degrees of intimacy. Thus, in the end it was decided to record whether or not respondents perceived themselves as having friends in any of the ethnic groups.

As might be expected, the majority of respondents said that they found most of their friends among their own ethnic group. It may give some encouragement, however, to those who hope for a more tolerant society that we are able to say that there was a substantial tendency among the sample to form inter-ethnic friendships.

Interview data cast additional light on the way that friendships were formed and maintained. What was clear was the importance of the school environment in encouraging it or discouraging it. Female interviewees seemed to have been more able than males to form inter-ethnic relationships at school. A Chinese female might have spoken for others from all ethnic groups when she said:

> I enjoyed my time there. Loved it. Do it again tomorrow. I got on with
> everyone. It was all right because it wasn't really, well, like no one used

to call each other. If you were friends you would just remain friends if you were black, white, green, purple.

However, it was not true for all as this Caribbean female makes clear:

Interviewer: How did you get on with pupils from other ethnic groups?
Interviewee: All right. There was a bit of racial stuff but there are racial problems everywhere. I mean, it might start off in school. You see more bullying and names being called in school. That's where it starts and that's where you learn black from white. That's where you're going to learn it from. It's up to the parents or the teachers to say what's right and what's wrong.

Male interviewees were much more guarded about their experiences. A Pakistani male who had recently left school described his experience:

Interviewer: So mostly you play games with your friends. What origin are those friends?
Interviewee: Predominantly Asian. But when I was at school I played badminton and my partner was a white pupil. He was in my class and I'd known him from the first year. And there was another one who was white.
Interviewer: Do you think the school encouraged 'mixed' partners?
Interviewee: All I can say is that they didn't encourage it but they didn't *dis*courage it. But what really happens, and it seems purely natural, that Asian kids will go towards Asian kids and white kids will go towards white kids.
Interviewer: So there's not this integration we hear about?
Interviewee: I don't think we'll have true integration.
Interviewer: Why do you think this is?
Interviewee: Because the white man is more hostile to non-white people than non-white people are towards white people.
Interviewer: Do you think black people can be racist?
Interviewee: No, I wouldn't say 'racist.' I would say 'defensive'.

Another person, a male Caribbean, described his experience of attending a school which had served a largely white, middle-class area:

When I first went there, there weren't many black guys there and the black guys that were there went around together. The white guys kept to themselves and the black guys kept to themselves and everything was all right. But if the two got together there was usually a fight.

And there were like 'cocks of the school' and 'cocks of the year' and stuff like that. And like there were two 'cocks of the school', one black and one white. Everyone was disputing the fact. The white guys said the black guy wasn't cock and vice versa.

Sometimes it all got pretty heated and on quite a few occasions the headmaster was called in to sort of calm us down . . .

Interviewer: Did you have any white friends at school?

Interviewee: Apart from the ones that were in my class, I didn't mingle with them. I kept myself to myself more . . . I had friends who were white, but, 'friends' — they'd got limitations. There were things I wouldn't tell white friends that I'd tell black friends.

The problem of mature arrivals is well defined by this Caribbean interviewee:

Coming from Jamaica, I think friendship would naturally grow up in the community where you both lived and so you became friends almost without knowing it. Because I came over here at a later age, then I didn't bother to actually go out and create that sort of friendship again, because it was like something lost. So you couldn't actually go out and find it. And I find that, since I've been over here, I've tended to relate better to people of my own ethnic background. I mean, I never actually force myself to make friends with people from different backgrounds. I speak to Asians quite a lot but I wouldn't say I've actually got any close Asian friends at all.

White respondents had much less to say on the subject. In answer to questions like, 'How did you get on with black pupils at school?' they tended to respond with non-commital statements like:

All right

or,

There weren't many black or Asian pupils, just a small minority. It was that sort of area where I lived. Nothing to do with the school.

or,

Quite a lot of ethnic minorities — Asians and black kids. Didn't particularly get on with them. Didn't have much contact with them. In games I suppose we played together. They all did games with us.

The difference in the nature and content of these responses provides much evidence about the perceptions of racial issues as between the dominant and minority groups.

Clearly, opportunities to take part in many activities are constrained by the level of available economic resources. In formulating the questionnaire we considered how best to arrive at an estimate of the socio-economic status of the respondents. It was decided at an early stage that direct questions such as 'How much do you earn?' (or in the case of youngsters still at school or in full-time education) 'How much do your parents earn?' would be likely to alienate possible respondents, even if, in the case of younger people, they knew the answer. It was therefore considered more appropriate to ask what their occupation was and what sort of houses they lived in. In this way, it was hoped, some indications of relative economic well-being would emerge.

It was clear that the majority of the sample had little in the way of net disposable income. Only 70 (6.5 per cent) were in full-time employment with 352 (32.5 per cent) in part-time jobs. Another 420 (38.8 per cent) were either still at school or were full-time students and 240 (22.8 per cent) were either registered unemployed or worked full-time at home.

The occupations by ethnic origin were largely in line with the ages of the sample. Thus 43.4 per cent of Bangladeshis were at school or full-time students as were 97.5 per cent of Chinese. Among the more established populations 30.6 per cent of the white British and 34.7 per cent of the West Indians were either at school or full-time students. Clearly, so far as students — both those at school and those in some form of post-school education — are concerned, their ability to participate depended very much on a complex set of conditions which included the provisions made by their educational institutions and their parents' ability to provide financial support.

As a further indicator of family income we asked for the type of housing the respondents lived in. Over one-third lived in terraced and almost a third in semi-detached houses. Of those living in terraced houses, the Chinese and Pakistani communities, at 26.8 per cent and 27.9 per cent were the lowest and the Bangladeshi at 63.2 per cent was the highest. Other communities fell within the range 32.5–43.8 per cent. Of those living in semi-detached houses, the Bangladeshi (14.2 per cent), African (17.4 per cent) and East African Asian (12.5 per cent) were the communities with the lowest proportions, the remainder falling in the range 24.8–37.7 per cent. Only 16.2 per cent of the whole sample lived in detached houses. Looking at the ethnic groups, the East African Asians showed the highest proportion, though the actual numbers were small. They were closely followed by the much larger Pakistani group with 31.2 per cent, with the Caribbeans the lowest at 5.0 per cent. Flats and other accommodation accounted for less than 15 per cent of the sample.

Whilst these data are suggestive of the economic status of the respondents they do not, of themselves, give an unambiguous indication. Taken with the information on their occupations, however, it was clear that the major ethnic groups (including the white British) had much in common. They were likely to be unemployed or in part-time employment or in unwaged employment in the home and they were most likely to be living either in a terraced or semi-detached house. From this it might plausibly be suggested that the majority could be described as urban poor. Above and below the majority there were those, if we may assume that detached housing strongly suggests house ownership, who were relatively better off and those who were registered as unemployed whom we may assume to be among the poorest. Students in higher and further education presented a particular problem in that they might be in receipt of an award and so had some independent means whilst others might not. Those still at school would be dependent on their parents. We asked for information on parents' occupations but many respondents refused to reply or gave information which did not enable an assessment of parental income to be made.

Finally, we assumed that parenthood was likely to restrict the ability of respondents to engage in activities — particularly if they took them out of the home. We therefore asked respondents if they had children living at home with them. Of Pakistani respondents 37.7 per cent were parents (the highest proportion) followed by West Indians (36.4 per cent) Africans (30.0 per cent) and Bangladeshis (24.5 per cent). Of white British respondents 15.5 per cent were parents whilst the relative youth and occupations of the Chinese put them at the bottom of the list with only 7.7 per cent.

It seemed inevitable that the behaviours of all our respondents would be modified by a range of conditioning factors working upon them. Economic status allied to social class would have their effects. We sought also to discover something of their religious beliefs, including their own perceptions of the importance those beliefs had in determining what they did in their everyday lives. Tables 7(a) and 7(b) sets out the responses to the question 'How much do you think it [your religious belief] affects most of the things you do in your everyday life?'

Taking the male white British group first, and bearing in mind that some 40 per cent said that they were either agnostic or atheist, few said that religion was 'very important' though, if anything, the oldest age band (25–30) were the most likely to do so. More in all age bands said that it was 'important', a similar number thought it 'not very important' and the largest group were those who said it was of 'no importance'.

Comparing those responses with the Pakistani and Bangladeshi groups (who, as Table 6 demonstrated, were virtually 100 per cent Muslim) it is clear that the general tendency is reversed, with the majorities in both groups saying that religion is either 'very important' or 'important'. The Chinese responses resemble those of the white British except that the numbers of respondents were very small since some 60 per cent were unbelievers. Indians, with their more complex mixture of Hindus, Sikhs and Muslims gave responses which suggest that, as a group, their beliefs were more likely to rate as 'important' than anything else, with the proportions of those rating them as 'very' and 'not very' important being about the same. Similarly, the Caribbean group responded that religion (almost certainly Christianity) was 'important', with a smaller proportion saying that it was 'very important' and somewhat fewer saying that it was of little or no importance. Again, it should be born in mind in assessing these results, that some 30 per cent of all Caribbeans said that they were unbelievers.

Female respondents show a slightly different pattern. White British females

Table 7(a): Importance Attached to Religious Belief by Ethnic Origin by Age and by Gender: Males

		Bang	Afr	Caribb	Chin	EAA	Ind	Pak	W/Brit
Very important	1*	11	2	2	–	1	8	12	1
	%+	37.9	20.0	16.7	–	20.0	24.2	52.2	3.0
	2*	9	1	4	7	–	5	7	2
	%+	50.0	12.5	30.8	30.4	–	13.9	50.0	5.9
	3*	7	3	4	5	–	5	5	5
	%	53.8	50.0	22.2	45.5	–	21.7	38.5	18.5
Important	1	8	4	4	4	1	10	7	4
	%	27.6	40.0	33.3	13.3	20.0	30.3	30.4	12.1
	2	2	2	5	3	1	11	4	7
	%	11.1	25.0	38.5	13.0	50.0	30.6	28.6	20.6
	3	3	2	4	–	–	8	3	3
	%	23.1	33.3	22.2	–	–	34.8	23.1	11.1
Not very important	1	5	3	1	4	–	8	3	5
	%	17.2	30.0	8.3	13.3	–	24.2	13.0	15.2
	2	5	5	2	1	1	9	2	3
	%	27.8	62.5	15.4	4.3	50.0	25.0	14.3	8.8
	3	3	–	7	–	2	2	4	5
	%	23.1	–	38.9	–	22.2	8.7	30.8	18.5
No importance	1	–	1	2	5	3	5	1	13
	%	–	10.0	16.7	16.7	60.0	15.2	4.3	39.4
	2	2	–	–	–	–	7	–	10
	%	11.1	–	–	–	–	19.7	–	29.4
	3	–	1	2	1	5	3	–	2
	%	–	16.7	11.1	9.1	55.6	13.0	–	7.4

* Band 1 covers ages 16–20; band 2 covers 21–25; band 3 covers age 26–30.
+ The percentages give the proportion of respondents in each ethnic group giving that level of importance to their belief. Thus, 37.9 per cent of Bangladeshis aged 16–20 saw their religion as 'Very important', 27.6 per cent as 'Important', 17.2 per cent as 'Not very important', and none as of 'No importance'. The percentages include unbelievers and those who declined to answer.

seemed more likely than males to attach a higher importance to their belief, though the numbers in the 'very important' and 'important' categories barely reached the 25 per cent mark and were frequently well below. For Bangladeshi and Pakistani females, over 70 per cent of all age groups saw religion as either 'very important' or 'important' and, unlike the males, this was also true for the Indians. The pattern for Caribbean females was similar to that for males with, if anything, a suggestion that for them religion was slightly more of a determinant to their behaviour. The numbers of Chinese responding were so small as to provide no secure basis for comment except that, for the few who had a belief, it did seem to have an importance.

At the level of general comment, it would seem that religion — whichever it was — was more likely to be important to females than males; that age (at any rate in the range 16–30) did not significantly affect the force of that belief; and that of the major religions, Islam was the most likely to be of real significance to its believers of either gender or at any age.

Table 7(b): Importance Attached to Religious Belief by Ethnic Origin by Age and by Gender: Females

		Bang	Afr	Caribb	Chin	EAA	Ind	Pak	W/Brit
Very important	1*	8	2	5	2	–	4	13	7
	%+	30.8	22.2	19.2	4.0	–	20.0	33.3	18.4
	2*	7	–	5	3	–	7	6	10
	%	63.6	–	18.5	21.4	–	26.9	31.6	25.6
	3*	5	1	6	–	1	2	14	4
	%	71.4	33.3	27.3	–	100.0	22.2	40.0	13.8
Important	1	10	2	7	14	1	11	12	7
	%	38.5	22.2	26.9	28.0	25.0	55.0	30.8	18.4
	2	3	3	4	1	–	8	9	5
	%	27.3	33.3	14.8	7.1	–	30.8	47.4	12.8
	3	–	2	9	–	–	5	11	3
	%	–	66.7	40.9	–	–	55.6	31.4	10.3
Not very important	1	5	1	4	8	1	2	7	9
	%	19.2	11.1	15.4	16.0	25.0	10.0	17.9	23.7
	2	–	–	5	–	–	5	1	8
	%	–	–	18.5	–	–	19.2	5.3	20.5
	3	–	–	3	–	–	–	6	5
	%	–	–	13.6	–	–	–	17.1	17.2
No importance	1	1	1	3	2	1	3	4	5
	%	3.8	11.1	11.5	4.0	25.0	15.0	10.3	13.2
	2	–	1	4	1	–	2	1	3
	%	–	11.1	14.8	7.1	–	7.7	5.3	7.7
	3	–	–	–	1	–	1	3	5
	%	–	–	–	20.0	–	11.1	8.6	17.2

* Band 1 covers ages 16–20; band 2 covers 21–25; band 3 covers ages 26–30.
+ The percentages give the proportion of respondents in each ethnic group giving that level of importance to their belief. Thus, 30.8 per cent of Bangladeshis aged 16–20 saw their religion as 'Very important', 38.5 per cent as 'Important', 19.2 per cent as 'Not very important', and 3.8 per cent as of 'No importance'. The percentages include unbelievers and those who declined to answer.

This view gained some support from the interviews which were conducted with volunteers from the original sample. Whilst the impact of religion was not a deliberate subject for discussion, the subject arose from time to time in the course of the interview. The comment on the relative impact of religions on different groups made by a Sikh female summarizes much that was said by others:

I feel that all the white people I know aren't religiously inclined at all. I mean they'd go to church on Sunday and that's it. 'God?' They'd never mention the word unless it was a joke. I mean, with Sikhs and Muslims and Hindus I can really discuss religion, because they know mine and I know theirs and that's what makes me feel so different to white folks. That, I feel, is what makes the difference between me and them, and their culture and my culture. I don't really see white culture existing really. I can't really see anything strong there, you know.

It is significant that, for her, religious belief defined a community's culture. Her own experience and that of her fellow South Asians made it impossible for her to see how a culture could cohere without the powerful unifying influence of a commonly-held religious belief to give it form and substance.

A Bangladeshi Muslim touched on the subject in the course of describing how she chose her friends. Her close friends were Asian, she said, because:

> Generally I think I choose my friends very carefully and I like them to have the same kind of values and opinions that I have. I think it's because of the religion that I am. I like to have friends from the same background.

How far religious beliefs might affect the day-to-day behaviours of their adherents, whether the teaching of Islam was of particular significance, and how far it could be attributed to the nature of Muslim societies was another question to which we addressed ourselves. We also looked at the extent to which people with other beliefs and from other ethnic groups responded to a range of societal pressures.

To do this we asked respondents to indicate the degree of importance they attached to the approval of parents, religious teachers, brothers and sisters, friends and the community at large when they contemplated doing anything. We stress here that we assume that their responses were as applicable to sport and recreation as to any other activity they might have wished to engage in. Their responses to other questions relating to social and leisure activities encourage the belief that this was a reasonable assumption. We then broke down their responses by ethnic group and gender, and into the three age bands (16–20, 21–25, 26–30). It will be recognized that analysis at this level of detail meant that the numbers in each category are inevitably small. We therefore preface our comments by saying that the results cannot, in detail, be regarded as conclusive. We believe, however, that, taken as a whole, they are suggestive of the level of social constraint under which respondents felt themselves to operate.

The responses to the question on parental approval indicate that, broadly speaking, this was the social factor which was most likely to affect the behaviour of respondents from all ethnic groups, both genders and from all three age bands. Females were more likely than males to say that parental approval was either 'very important' or 'important' and this tendency appeared more strongly in the 16–20 year olds than in the older respondents. Thus, of 16–20 year-old males, 90 per cent of Pakistanis, 80 per cent of Bangladeshis and a similar proportion of West Indians said that parental approval was either 'very important' or 'important'. For females of the same ages, the proportions rose to 91 per cent for Pakistanis, 88 per cent for Bangladeshis but fell to 64 per cent for West Indians. For the Chinese the responses were still high both for males (55 per cent) and females (64.6 per cent). There was a quite sharp distinction in the responses of Indian males (55 per cent) and females (83 per cent). A similar difference was found between white British males (27.5 per cent) and females (57.1 per cent).

For the respondents aged between 21–25, a similar pattern held: 80 per cent of Bangladeshi males and 70 per cent of females, and 74 per cent of Pakistani males (88 per cent of females) looked for parental approval. Only 53.6 per cent of Indian males but 70.8 per cent of females did so. For white British males the proportion fell to 6.6 per cent and for females to 36.1 per cent. Other ethnic group responses also fell by comparison with the younger respondents — usually by about 20 per cent.

Respondents aged 26–30 showed a marked reduction in the need for parental approval, with some notable exceptions. Indian males still found it important as did Pakistani (77.4 per cent), Indian (66.6 per cent) and Bangladeshi females (75.0 per cent).

Interview data provided similar insights. Thus, a Pakistani female talked about growing up in Britain and the restraints she felt she experienced that were imposed by her parents. It was also interesting to see how she reflected on her current position and attributed her change of attitude to increased maturity and understanding.

> When I was younger, English people used to go for dancing and things like that and I couldn't do those things because my parents didn't approve of it, which I would have liked to do at that time. But now that I'm older, and have more understanding, I'm not interested. At that time my parents prevented me. They didn't think it was right according to our religion. Now I'm not interested. I've got other interests. I've got my children, I'm happy with them, I've got other interests. I'm too busy to think of things like that any more. And I understand my religion a lot better now.

It was also interesting to hear how different ethnic and religious groups from South Asia saw the variations in parental control from one community to another and between the genders.

Interviewer: Do you think they're different?
Interviewee: Their parents [of Muslim friends] are very strict I think. They don't go out as often as I do . . . I mean out on their own or with friends. They usually go out with family, if they go anywhere. They do get to go out with each other in groups, to parties and things like that. But only for a limited amount of time. Not really freely — like 'Mum I'm going out for a minute.' It's not that easy. They more or less have to have permission before they go out. There are some families that aren't as restrictive, but there are quite a lot where, you know, the parents are over-protective of their daughters.

Not of the sons! Definitely not. I mean it's — some of them are out everywhere, going here or there, gallivanting around wherever. I think, in the Muslim community in particular, there's a lot of lads who are out

in the cars being free and wild and going to night clubs and everything
— and the daughters are at home cooking; the same old routine over
and over. I mean they're the ones who are just sitting in all the time
really. Just all the responsibilities I think. No sort of freedom . . .

[About friends] Some friends rebelled actually and they've gone out and
done things they shouldn't have done. Some have rebelled, girls from my
class [when she was at school] for instance, but I mean, that's really the
parents' fault. In the end it's always the parents that get hurt. Why did
they do it? Why did they do it? It's like tying them down and not letting them go here and there. Being over-protective. Questioning them
all the time, you know. Not letting them have the freedom to do what
they want. Not letting them say what they want. Being very authoritative
over them all the time.

It is important, though, not to assume that all Muslim females are over-
protected by their parents. Higher levels of education and social class generally
seem to result in greater freedom to children. Thus a Bengali female talked of
how her relationship with her parents developed in these terms.

As long as I got there safely and I got home safely, they were fine about
it — and they knew where I was. Yes I do realize now [that they were
unusual]. I didn't at the time, because I was brought up with English
friends . . . It's just that I've been brought up differently.
Interviewer: Your mum and dad have no problems with the kinds of
worries that many other parents have?
Interviewee: No. Not really. They've got a lot of trust in me. And I've
earned that trust as well! As long as you can show them, and show a lot
of respect for each other. And I'm happy, so they're happy. And rather
than lay the law down that's the way I've been brought up . . .

The majority of the girls living in [this area] are from the Sylhet District
whereas my parents are from Dacca, which is the city.

Other respondents were less fortunate. One Indian female who had led a
relatively free life whilst at home with her parents had recently been married and
had moved into her husband's parents' household.

Interviewer: Since you got married, do you do nothing [in the way of
physical activities] at all?
Interviewee: Not really, no. I don't really have the time now. Not
just the time, I think. Because of the environment I'm in now. Like I
said, there weren't so many restrictions with my mum, before, on doing
anything outside work hours or school hours. Whereas now, I've moved
into a different family and they're a lot more strict. I don't think

they'd actually approve if I went out and did these things on my own . . . Because, I don't know, it's just that they're old-fashioned.

Interviewer: Don't they see sport as something that is an important part of your life?

Interviewee: No, because I'm female, that sort of stereotyping comes into it, and because I'm Asian . . . The only other person is the younger daughter and she's ten and she does because she does it at school and she's doing all her activities there. But I've never seen her go out to a sports centre.

I'd love to take my sister-in-law (the younger one) and maybe my brother-in-law out to do things like ten-pin bowling, and they've got a skating rink just a couple of minutes away from the house, but it's just not seen as the 'normal' thing to do; it's not the right thing to do, according to them . . .

Interviewer: When do you think you'll be able to do that?

Interviewee: When I've got my own space. Maybe when I'm living on my own, I can do the sort of things I want to. Whereas now, like I said, mainly because of the family . . . I'm in that for a while, but, then, when I get my own house, I can carry on and do what I want to. There'll be no restriction — well, not many restrictions then.

It would perhaps be a useful moment to touch on the perceptions of white British society and culture as perceived by members of ethnic minority groups whom we interviewed. Asian females, particularly, commented on the freedom enjoyed by their white peers to do pretty much what they wanted compared to their own more regulated lives. As one Indian put it:

I'm always seeking the permission of my parents. I have to ask them, whereas they just do what they want.

Combined with this perception of the greater freedom of white people went a perception of irresponsibility. South Asians were almost unanimous in this.

I think they [a lot of white people of my age] act very irresponsible. They're very free and a lot of people I know smoke and I disapprove of that. And they drink. And they really ruin their health. They're not really responsible enough, I think.

Having said this, many also made it clear that they did not claim the right to sit in judgment. Many echoed this interviewee:

We are different communities. We behave according to our lifestyle and they behave according to theirs.

For Afro-Caribbeans it was the similarity rather than any differences that they seized upon:

> . . . most of the white people. I mean that I mingle about with, it's like they're no different from me. The only thing that's different is the colour and that doesn't say anything for me now, because it's like we're all one.

One Chinese reflected on her white peers' relative freedom and self-confidence.

> I think most of the English friends I know have more self-confidence than Chinese. I think the way they're brought up is different, their culture is different. They've got a sense of freedom. They really believe that personal freedom is very important and they don't care about other people's attitude towards them. So it's quite different from Chinese people, because Chinese that I know care a lot about other people's attitudes. They will think about other people's attitudes towards this, so they take other people's attitudes into consideration when they make a decision — even though the decision is quite personal.

For another, it was the sexual mores of the whites that distinguished them from the Chinese — an issue raised more than once by respondents from other ethnic groups.

> One thing that crosses my mind is that they view sex in a very different way. They are more open-minded about such issues. We tend to keep to tradition . . . It's not that I dislike this attitude towards sex. It's just that we were brought up very differently in this respect . . . It's their culture after all, but it's different from ours.

Yet another Chinese female took a more relaxed view about the whole thing.

> Most of my friends aren't religious and I'm not religious. We're just alike really. I think, because I've been brought up here and my friends have been with me all my life, most of them I've known since I was about four years old, we don't behave any differently.

> Culture? I don't have any. It's just sometimes we watch Chinese videos and I speak Chinese. The only difference between me and my friends is that my family background is Chinese and their family background is English, or Asian, or whatever.

The subject of parental control did not frequently arise with males and when it did, the interview usually supported the views expressed earlier on the subject of the relative freedom of the males. A Muslim male on a full-time course of study put it this way:

Interviewer: How much effect do you think your parents have on your activities?

Interviewee: My parents see that I'm getting a good education so they allow me to socialize. They wouldn't really mind if I came home at three o'clock in the morning and said nothing about it. They trust me, you know. They know I'm not going to go off fooling around. They did encourage me to study more rather than doss around . . . All I can say is they don't *dis*approve.

If the above responses are compared with those resulting from the question about the need for the approval of religious teachers, the differences are quite marked. Responses from males aged between 16–20 showed that about half the number who would take their parents opinions into account do so for religious teachers. Thus 45 per cent of Bangladeshis and 42 per cent of Pakistanis said that this was a 'very important' or 'important' consideration as did 37.5 per cent of West Indians and 28.8 per cent of Indians. Notably, not one of the white British group did so.

Among the females of the same ages, the responses were higher than for males but still significantly lower than for parental approval. Of the major minority groups, Bangladeshis (63.6 per cent — all of them in the 'very important' category) gave it the most importance. They were followed by Pakistanis (39.4 per cent) and Indians (33.4 per cent). The small numbers of Africans in this group make their response of 71.5 per cent unreliable. White British respondents (37.5 per cent) compare sharply with the response from males and are perhaps higher than might be expected.

In the 21–25 age band, the picture for males is much as for the younger respondents. No white British respondent attached any significance to the opinions of their religious teachers. Pakistani (40.0 per cent) and Bangladeshi respondents (35.7 per cent) were most affected. The numbers of females in this age band was small and it would be sensible not to place too much significance on the results obtained (Pakistanis 41.2 per cent showing the greatest influence) were it not for the fact that females aged between 26–30, where the numbers involved are higher, maintain a general similarity of pattern. There, 46.9 per cent of the Pakistani female respondents said that religious teachers' opinions were either 'very important' or 'important', followed by 42.9 per cent of Indians. Males of that age group also showed a level of conformity which is little different from those of the youngest age group — Indians 53.3 per cent, Bangladeshis 37.5 per cent (though, again, the numbers involved are very small.)

Thus, in general terms, it seems possible to say that the influence of religious teachers on all respondents from the minority groups was markedly less than that of parents but that those groups who were predominantly Muslims seemed to take account of them than those who were not. In this there seemed to be no significant differences between the genders or between the age bands.

Responses to our question on the level of influence exerted by siblings suggested that, in general, their effect on males was fairly trivial. For white

British respondents, particularly in the younger age bands, they seemed of no account. Of the minority groups, Pakistani, Indian, Chinese and Bangladeshis showed a fairly constant response at around 30 per cent. For the females they had a slightly larger impact but the differences remained insignificant.

The influence of friends' approval was of interest in that, generally speaking, both for males and females and at all age ranges, the white British group seemed as influenced as the ethnic minority groups. However, as with sibling influence, that of friends was small compared with that of parents and religious teachers.

Community influence again had little effect. Even among communities where approval by peers might be expected to be a force to be reckoned with, only small numbers of respondents said they were affected. However, it may be that community influence was transmitted through parents, who, as we have seen, can figure largely.

Be that as it may, some respondents saw community influence as a force to be reckoned with — particularly the females — though the kinds of attitudes were seen to change, even within the same ethnic group, from one area to another. Here a Pakistani Muslim speaks of her experience.

> I don't know. The thing is, the attitudes of people [living] in this area. I don't think they'll change. There's no communication between the younger generation and the older. And I think that's the root cause of the problems of them being over-protective of the kids. There's just too much of a communication gap. To be honest, I think it's getting worse. Because now, I can see those sort of attitudes rubbing off on our generation. It's not getting easier for girls to get out. I think it's getting worse.
> **Interviewer**: Why?
> **Interviewee**: Stereotyping, sexism. Just, the attitudes of society I think. In our sort of culture, we lay a lot of emphasis on what society thinks, what other people think, all the time.

Some, on the evidence of one interviewee, managed to come to terms with community disapproval and do most of the things they wanted, subject to their perception of what was permitted by their religious belief.

> **Interviewer**: Do you think other Muslim women envy the kinds of freedom you've got?
> **Interviewee**: I think they're shocked more than anything. They look back and think 'Why's she allowed to do all these things?'
> **Interviewer**: Shocked as in disapproving?
> **Interviewee**: Yes, at first disapproving and then after, maybe, envious.

To revert then to the question posed earlier: was it religious belief that was the main determinant of general and social behaviour in predominantly Muslim (and other) groups, or were other factors involved? On the basis of the evidence we were able to collect, it is possible to suggest that the authority exerted by parents (and perhaps we may add, other senior members of the family) in ethnic minority communities generally, was greater than is customary in white British families of the same socio-economic class. Further, it seemed that this authority was given greatest respect by those minorities who were predominantly Muslim. That, in fact, the two factors modifying behaviour — Islam and parental authority — were closely intertwined but none the less distinct. The authority might take its justification from the belief and be supported in greater or lesser degree by other issues, such as the need to conform to the expectations of sub-groups within the community, but it was the relationship between the senior and junior members of the family which was most effective in determining the actions of young people. It was through the parents that these pressures to conform to the societal norms of the community were applied to the children.

Further, it underlined the dominant position of parents and other male relatives over women in these societies. The distinction between the expectations applied to Muslim males and females was well expressed in two of the interviews quoted above. The following comments made by a British-born Pakistani male in relation to the activities of the local social services department throws additional light.

> A lot of the elders, [senior male members of the local community] they think a lot of these English ladies, what's doing the project or whatever, their ideas are not so good. They think the ideas the English women are giving are outside their culture. It will give their women different ideas. They'll think about more freedom. They try to confine them. They try not to let them have too much knowledge. So what they do, they try to keep them, like in a box you know, and not let them get out. I think that's what it is.

We consider some of the issues that arise from the relationship of parents and children in ethnic minority communities at greater length later.

The direct effects of belief on the actions of adherents were negligible. The need for the approval of religious teachers, though less significant than that of parents, was second only in determining behaviour. (Indeed, for the white British group it was very much more significant — the Biblical requirement to 'honour thy father and thy mother' seemed to form no part of the white respondents' behaviour patterning.)

Leisure Activities

In order to place their sporting activities into their general leisure context, respondents were asked to write down all the things they *enjoyed* doing in their leisure time. Examples such as 'talking to friends' and 'day-dreaming' were

Table 8(a): Leisure Activities by Ethnic Origin and by Gender: Males

Activities	Bang	Afr	Caribb	Chin	EAA	Ind	Pak	W/Brit	Other	Totals
Social	26	16	22	35	8	51	22	54	5	239
%*	24.3	23.2	19.8	18.0	28.6	19.5	22.9	21.1	–	21.1
Sports	35	16	36	64	12	102	34	80	9	387
%	32.7	23.2	32.4	33.0	42.9	39.1	35.4	31.3	–	34.1
Arts	–	5	4	10	–	10	1	13	–	44
%	–	7.2	3.6	5.7	–	3.8	1.0	5.1	–	3.9
Domestic	4	2	6	10	2	13	10	11	1	55
%	3.7	2.9	5.4	5.2	7.1	5.0	7.3	4.3	–	4.8
Religious	–	2	4	2	–	7	1	6	–	22
%	–	2.9	3.6	1.0	–	2.7	1.0	2.3	–	1.9
Passive	22	22	25	45	5	58	25	81	6	298
%	29.9	31.9	22.5	23.2	17.9	22.2	26.0	31.6	–	26.3
Education	–	2	1	13	–	7	–	2	2	26
%	–	2.9	0.9	6.7	–	2.7	–	0.8	–	2.3
Non-Active	4	2	2	8	–	2	2	1	–	21
%	3.7	2.9	1.8	4.1	–	0.8	2.1	0.4	–	1.9
Travel	3	2	9	5	1	8	4	7	1	40
%	2.8	2.9	8.1	2.6	3.6	3.1	4.2	2.7	–	3.5
Ethnic Centre	2	–	–	–	–	1	–	–	–	3
%	0.2	–	–	–	–	0.1	–	–	–	0.2

* The percentage figures were arrived at by grossing up all the activities cited by the members of that ethnic group and expressing the number of times the particular type of activity was cited as a proportion of the whole.

given as an indication that we wanted to know what they really did and were not likely to make any judgments on the nature of their responses. The results are contained in Tables 8(a) and 8(b).

Before commenting on their contents, we expand a little on the nature of the activities included under each heading.

Social	includes visiting friends, going to the pub, entertaining at home.
Sports	includes all sporting and recreational activities listed on page 6 of the questionnaire.
Arts	includes all arts-related activities such as drawing, painting, photography, visiting art galleries.
Domestic	includes normal activities about the house and embroidery, sewing and DIY.
Religious	includes religious observation and social work.
Passive	includes watching TV, listening to the radio/Hifi, going to the cinema, spectating.
Education	includes homework, attendance at evening classes, Open University.
Non-Active	includes all non-physical games such as board- and table-games, cards, crosswords and the like.
Travel	as normally understood.
Ethnic C	was reserved for specific references to visiting the ethnic centre.

Table 8(b): Leisure Activities by Ethnic Origin and by Gender: Females

Activities	Bang	Afr	Caribb	Chin	EAA	Ind	Pak	W/Brit	Other	Totals
Social	28	12	52	43	7	27	61	94	5	329
%*	30.8	19.4	20.7	20.8	21.9	17.6	24.6	25.8	–	23.6
Sports	9	18	65	52	9	36	27	88	2	306
%	9.9	29.0	25.9	25.1	28.1	23.5	10.9	24.1	–	21.9
Arts	4	4	14	14	1	9	6	24	–	76
%	4.4	6.5	5.6	6.8	3.1	5.9	2.4	6.6	–	5.4
Domestic	8	4	27	19	1	20	48	24	1	152
%	8.8	6.5	10.8	9.2	3.1	13.1	19.4	6.6	–	10.9
Religious	–	–	6	1	4	3	4	12	–	30
%	–	–	2.4	0.5	12.5	2.0	1.6	3.3	–	2.2
Passive	38	17	76	60	8	51	81	98	2	431
%	41.8	27.4	30.3	29.0	25.0	33.3	32.7	26.8	–	30.9
Education	–	2	1	5	–	3	9	1	–	21
%	–	3.2	0.4	2.4	–	2.0	3.6	0.3	–	1.5
Non-Active	4	1	2	3	–	1	1	2	–	14
%	4.4	1.6	0.8	1.4	–	0.7	0.4	0.5	–	1.0
Travel	–	3	3	5	2	2	6	9	1	31
%	–	4.8	1.2	2.4	6.3	1.3	2.4	2.5	–	2.2
Ethnic Centre	–	–	–	–	–	1	1	3	–	5
%	–	–	–	–	–	0.7	0.4	0.8	–	0.4

* The percentage figures were arrived at by grossing up all the activities cited by the members of that ethnic group and expressing the number of times the particular type of activity was cited as a proportion of the whole.

The method of arriving at the percentage figures in the tables was chosen because it was felt that it would best represent the balance of activities enjoyed by each ethnic group.

Taking Table 8(a) giving the results for males first, and looking at the totals for all activities, it is clear that sports activities are the most popular (34.1 per cent of all activities cited) followed by passive (26.3 per cent) and socializing (21.1 per cent). Beside these, all others fell into insignificance. Sports were most frequently cited by the Bangladeshi, Caribbean, Chinese, East African Asian, Indian and Pakistani respondents, and as second by the African and white British. Six groups gave passive activities as either their first or second choice.

Table 8(b) gives the results for females. The totals for all activities give passive (30.9 per cent) as first, social (23.6 per cent) second and sports (21.9 per cent) third, although a convincing fourth, domestic (10.9 per cent) is not negligible. Only the African and East African Asian groups gave passive activities second place, all the rest made it first. Whereas the male respondents showed little variation in the levels of their responses, the females showed some noteworthy variations. Thus, Bangladeshis were 10 per cent more likely to be engaged in some passive occupation than any other group, gave the lowest response to sports, the highest to social and (for all practical purposes) enjoyed domestic occupations as much as sporting activities. Pakistani females gave a very similar response to sport (10.9 per cent) as the Bangladeshis (9.9 per cent) and were twice as likely to cite domestic occupations (19.4 per cent) as sporting activities. Indeed, the general patterns of response by these two groups have much in common. Indian women, too, gave a substantial response (13.1 per cent) to domestic matters. Only African and East African Asian respondents gave sports as their first choices, Caribbean and Indian as their second, Bangladeshi and white British as third and for Pakistanis it fell to fourth. Generally speaking, therefore, sport formed a substantially smaller part of the leisure activities for women than it did for men and this difference was accentuated if comparisons are made between males and females of the same ethnic group.

Reviewing the responses given during interviews, it was clear that the most privileged group, so far as the quantity of free time was concerned, was the students. This was true both for those at school and for those on some form of post-school course. For the latter group, they not only had more free time but a much greater control over its distribution through the day. They were also unique in that they had fewer responsibilities for maintaining themselves. Thus, for example, a respondent of Caribbean origin and a full-time student, describes his free time activities:

> In my free time I play some sports — cricket at weekends during the summer. A couple of friends who live in the same neighbourhood as I do, we gather together and play on a piece of land and we play — not competitive sport but just for fun. I also play badminton sometimes . . . Apart from that, when I work up at the Youth Club, I play sports with the kids.

> A normal weekend would be playing cricket on a Sunday. Probably on a Saturday night we would go to the club. During the day on Saturday I'd probably go round the shops.

Or a female Chinese full-time student:

> Last weekend — what did I do? Oh yes. On Saturday we went weight training and then we went swimming. And then after, we met up again and went to a disco that night. On Sunday, after I went home I went to my friend's house — I can't remember really. Probably watched a football match.

Next most privileged in terms of free time were the males. This remained true across the ethnic groups and regardless of age, religious affiliation, or marital and economic status. Thus a Caribbean male in full-time work:

> My free time is what's left after I've finished work. What I do is power lifting and weight training.

> Saturdays is basically for training. After training [last Saturday] I went out in the evening to the pictures. And on Sundays in the morning until

about twelve o'clock I was at home, and then I went down to the club, watching some other guys and helping them out.

Similarly an unemployed white British adult:

Yesterday, went to sign on. Messed about the house: doing a bit of decorating at the moment. Went to a mate's house and then to the pub.

At weekends [I] mainly go to football matches, then go to the pub at night time. Did that last weekend. Free time is all the time.

As in the interviews cited above, males occasionally spoke of going 'to' or 'round' the shops, but never of 'doing the shopping.' The last interview was cited because it was the only one recorded in which a male referred to any domestic activity.

Females who were not students were the least favoured group. Those with children seemed to have little free time and even less opportunity to do what they wanted with it. A Caribbean woman speaking of her free time had this to say:

You don't have free time when you've got kids in the way . . . Well, I don't think I've got free time anyway, apart from two-and-a-half hours when she's at the nursery — and I don't think that's enough.
Interviewer: So what you're saying to me is that you have no free time. No time for yourself. No time to do what you enjoy — to go to places — no time at all!
Interviewee: Sometimes I do get time but, because I don't go out that often, I think 'What's the point of going out anyway, because I don't go out and I don't meet anyone new anyway . . .' So I stay in, even though the kids aren't here sometimes.

Another Caribbean with a part-time job told a similar story:

I don't often get much free time because there's so much to do . . . I wake up at 7.30, then I have to get A— up and T— [her sons]. Get them off to school. I leave home about quarter past nine to get to work for ten o'clock. Then, after work there's the shopping to do and I look after a friend's child during the afternoon. And [her own children] leave school at three thirty and come home. So, as you can see, my hands are really full.
Every alternate weekend I go into work. When I get back home it's the same routine to keep the house together. On Sundays I attend church in the morning and in the evening.
Interviewer: Do you do any leisure activities at the moment?
Interviewee: No. Not at all.

Interviewer: If you *really* wanted to, could you?

Interviewee: I don't see that I've really got the time. Maybe I'm making excuses that I haven't got the time. Because I'm quite a sturdy person and I'm very conscious of my weight and my figure, so I wouldn't like to be seen in public, semi-naked, doing anything.

From the interview it was not clear whether her concern about her 'sturdy' figure came from a reluctance to be seen by men or by other women. We can, however, record that there were a number of instances of women who found the presence of men embarrassing to the point where they chose not to engage in a range of activities. Moreover, this situation was not restricted to any ethnic group, nor did it have much to do with the sturdiness of their figures. There were examples of women from all ethnic groups, religions and physical configurations who found it distasteful to be inspected by males as if they were potential properties.

Women without children enjoyed rather more freedom. A typical example of the kind was this white British respondent:

Free time for me is the time when I'm not working and I'm not looking after my flat or my dog. I spend it usually, by seeing my friends or going out with them. Or I go to the gym on my own; see my parents; go to the cinema, concerts — things like that.

Last weekend I went shopping in the morning and then went over to my parents to go to the local hairdressers over there in the afternoon. In the evening my boyfriend called round and we went to Manchester for a few drinks and then to a club and stayed there all night dancing. And then, Sunday, I didn't particularly do much last Sunday. Spent the day mostly reading, tidying up, things like that. Most Sundays I go over to see my parents and then go out on Sunday evenings.

The most liberated Bengali female encountered during the study (and, incidentally, one with a record of sporting activities among the most impressive of all female respondents) told us

At the moment I'm not getting as much [chance to engage in physical activities] as I'd like to do because of the time limit. When you're running your own house as well it makes a big demand.

We do a lot of walking at the weekends. Last weekend we went to X Reservoir. We spend as much time walking as possible because we really enjoy that. And I go fishing with my brother and a few friends . . .

More typical was the account given by a married Indian with no children in full-time work:

I don't have much free time now within the household . . . So most of the free time I've got is spent working round the house really. On the odd occasions I've been out I've been to the pictures, but I've not really got as much free time as I did before I was married.

I used to go out quite a bit to the theatre and do sport, like badminton. Cinema, again, a lot more often, like twice a month. Whereas now, everything's a bit more restricted because I've got a lot more responsibility.

Interviewer: Before marriage you said you used to do all these things [activities]. Don't you have time now?

Interviewee: No. Not really, because the weekends — the only time I do get a large amount of time that's free, that's usually when we get invited to weddings and parties. So outside activities take up all my weekends.

The contrast between the kind of leisure time described by these women and those of the other groups was much more pronounced than between themselves as representatives of different ethnic groups. Their domestic responsibilities figured largely. Children substantially reduced their mobility but none of the males interviewed mentioned children as a constraint on their activities. Nor did any of the males mention visits to parents as part of their social duty. The extracts quoted above — as with many other interviews — show how women accepted these domestic, social and family duties as part of their lives. By comparison, the males presented themselves as grown-up children who were able to do pretty well whatever they wanted within the constraints of time, whilst the females shouldered all the responsibilities of social and domestic life.

There was little, if any, suggestion in our interviewees of the 'new man', cooperating with and sharing in the responsibilities of domesticity and thus contributing towards equality of opportunity in following leisure pursuits. This may have been a result of the nature of the sample. As demonstrated earlier, the number of middle-class professionals of either gender in it was very small.

Physical Fitness

Before dealing with the physical activities that the sample took part in, we report on their own assessments of current levels of fitness and what sort of ambitions they had to improve on them. It can be argued that self-assessed levels of fitness are highly subjective and we accept that this is so. However, it may be encouraging to note that for both males and females, the totals for each level of fitness approximate to the normal curve of distribution which is substantially what might be expected from a sample within the age range of this study. Perhaps it would be sensible to suggest that the levels of fitness claimed should not be regarded as absolute but comparative. Thus 'average' would come to mean 'about the same as most of the people I know', 'very fit' to mean 'very much fitter than most of the people I know' and so on.

With these caveats, it appears that the males of our sample reckoned themselves in general to be fitter than did the females and this was true of all ethnic groups (with the exception of East African Asians where the numbers are so small as to be unreliable). Of those claiming to be either 'above average' or 'very fit', males in all ethnic groups except Indians (29.9 per cent) fell in the range 40.9–63.9 per cent.

The proportion of females claiming this level of fitness was substantially lower than for males: if East African Asians are excluded, all fell within the range 19.7–38.1 per cent. Indian females again provided the group with the smallest claim. Although there was a substantial reduction in the proportion of females claiming this level of fitness as against males, it is interesting to note that there was a surprisingly close relationship between the males and females in each ethnic group (East African Asians excluded). Thus, ranking each ethnic group according to their assessment of fitness above the average and giving the ranking of males first, we find: Bangladeshis, 1:3; Africans, 2:2; Caribbeans, 6:6; Chinese, 7:7; Indians 8:8; Pakistanis 5:5; white British, 3:5. Those claiming 'average' fitness hovered around the 40 per cent mark for males and 55 per cent for females.

We then went on to ask, 'how fit you would like your body to be?'. The responses suggest that more males than females would like to be as 'fit as possible' but that a huge majority — 85.4 per cent of males and 87.0 per cent of females — would like to improve on their present level. Little difference existed between levels of ambition expressed by the ethnic groups. Pakistani and Bangladeshi males and females showed marginally less ambition than others and the Chinese, equally slightly, showed more, but these differences are inconclusive.

The association between desire for fitness and actual participation in sport and physical recreation was clearly of interest. Our results were obtained from a calculation of an *index of participation* and on more sophisticated statistical tests which are described at greater length later in this chapter.

For most males there was an increase in participation as the desire for fitness rose. The groups who wanted to be fitter did significantly more than those who were satisfied with their fitness. ($P < .01$ and $P < .05$) The 'don't care' group numbered only eight in total which explains why they did not figure in any significant differences. It is, of course, important to note that 374 out of the 439 (85 per cent) male respondents wanted to be fitter than they were, suggesting that fitness may be a reason for taking part though, as interview materials showed, not necessarily the prime reason.

An almost identical proportion of women (87 per cent) expressed a desire to be fitter than they were, but this desire for fitness did not differentiate actual participation as it had done for males. There was quite a wide range of participation ratings for each category of desire for fitness except 'don't care'. The fact that there were significant differences in participation between the female ethnic groups suggests that as desire for fitness increased, there was a much greater increase in actual participation among Chinese, white British and Caribbeans than there was among Bangladeshis and Pakistanis. The latter may have expressed almost as much desire for improved fitness as say, white British, but have not translated it into action, most probably for cultural reasons which have been described already. An alternative explanation could be that participation occurs for reasons other than fitness, eg. social interaction, but the fact that average participation rating rose as desire for fitness rose, with each ethnic group showing similar patterns, suggests that desire for fitness was indeed a reason for taking part. This view was confirmed in some of the interviews.

Age did not seem to affect the results materially for the females. The same ethnic group differences appeared in each of the age groups studied. Participation decreased as desire for fitness fell, except in the 21–25 age group where there was little variation across the desire-for-fitness levels. In each age group, desire to be at least fitter than they were remained high: 86 per cent among the under 20s; 92 per cent among the 21–25s; and 83 per cent among the over 25s.

When looking at the effects of religion and desire for fitness on participation among males, we had to draw the same conclusions as with ethnic groups, that is, that the only participation differences lay between levels of desire for fitness, rather than between religions. For females, differences in participation were also found between levels of desire for fitness, and between Muslims and Christians. But there was no significant interaction between religion and desire for fitness as there had been between ethnic groups and desire for fitness. It would seem then that cultural differences due to ethnicity interacted more with desire for fitness than did cultural differences due to religion, in affecting participation, as far as the females were concerned.

Respondents were asked *why* they took part in their current activities. Not surprisingly, many of them saw fitness, which they closely associated with health, as important. A white British female expressed it this way:

> Mainly I go swimming because, I have to say, I don't do any other exercise. I mean, I do quite like swimming but I don't know I would choose to do it if it wasn't a healthy exercise. I usually go with a friend and that's nice, for the company, but it's for health reasons really.

A Pakistani female said much the same, but, as it were, in a mirror image:

> **Interviewer**: Do you do anything to keep fit?
> **Interviewee**: Not really. I should be doing a lot of things because I am very unhealthy at the moment.

Respondents often gave other reasons for their activities, however, though fitness might be included, perhaps as a secondary reason. These comments, emphasizing the social aspects of sport and recreation were given in the course of an interview with an Indian female.

> But one thing I've always laid importance on is the socializing part. I think it's the best thing you get out of it. Not the competitive thing — winning; the socializing, when you go out and do that sort of thing.

I think health, but I think, more importantly, if you enjoy something, you should do that. Also it's relaxing. The most important thing for me is the team things; getting involved with other people in the team; mixing; socializing. That's how I see it.

A white British female was clear that, for her, the social aspect came first in her decision to return to sport. It was only after she started to play that health became an objective.

The first reason was a social reason. It's only in the last few years that I've tried to do things to be healthy.

For many women, across the ethnic boundaries, physical activities were seen as a way to look good and hence, to increase their self-confidence or improve their self-image. A white British female said it like this:

The main reason is to feel fit and healthy. I find I've benefited a lot from doing it. I've felt better and more energetic and a lot more toned-up. And my figure has improved in leaps and bounds. I just feel really healthy, which is something I've never felt before.

A Bengali female expressed similar ideas:

I think it's because it [badminton] is something I enjoy doing. Dancing is something I do for enjoyment. It's something I've always been interested in and wanted to do. It makes you feel a lot better health-wise. Generally, I think, exercise is something that can really help you to feel a lot better about yourself.

A Pakistani female had much the same to say:

I just generally want to feel healthier and fitter and tone up my body. It's [aerobics] a good way of exercising every muscle in your body that you have. And to look good, I suppose. To give myself a better image — stop putting the pounds on.

It was unusual for a female to say that the game or activity was the prime reason for taking part and even when she did, as this Chinese female did, she came to it after speaking of the other advantages:

I always think that after playing games I always feel very fresh and I can concentrate better on my studies. Besides that, especially for girls, you have to look out for your figure. I can lose weight as well. But that's not the main reason I play sport: the main reason would be because I enjoy playing them, basically.

It was also noteworthy that not one female interviewee saw winning as the prime objective. Indeed, some went out of their way to say that winning was irrelevant in their decision to take part.

Males, on the other hand, were much more likely to take part because of the sport itself and to want to win. A white British male was very clear on the subject:

> You play games for enjoyment. Not really for health and fitness. I suppose that comes into it but it's not the main reason. It's because you enjoy it, not because I'm going to be fit or anything like that. It's the game itself.

A Caribbean — a weight lifter — had this to say:

> Well, you see, one of my mates, by the time he was twenty-one, he had all these records. And yes, I'd like to be like that, but I didn't get into it until later than him, and when I did get into it, I like it. It was almost like a drug. You did a little bit and you wanted more.

Another person seemed to see fitness as a necessary evil to be achieved as a regrettable prerequisite to playing his game:

> Health and fitness is a very welcome bonus because I don't play to get fit. I mean, I don't train hard enough to be a really good rugby player so that I can get into the first team. I go and train with the other lads, running, trying to get some stamina and fitness up there, but it's not particularly interesting to me.

Whereas females spoke of the positive value of exercise as a means of improving their self-image, the only two males who touched on a related aspect saw its value in rather different terms. For them it had to do with the relief of stress, or the need to lose the tensions and frustrations of work. Both men were from the Caribbean community and one had this to say:

> **Interviewer**: Why did you play badminton?
> **Interviewee**: Get rid of a lot of the frustrations and tensions of the day at work. It kept me fit and it got me into an environment where people were.

The other:

> I play basically to relieve stress. I do weight training as well and I find that if I'm tense and under pressure from work and I go to the gym where I can work out, it relieves that tension. It's quite effective in that way. And when you're playing cricket you do a lot of running about and that also helps to relieve tension and keeps you fit.

Before looking at the sports and games played, we draw together the threads of the previous pages in which we have examined the priorities given to sport in general leisure activities, assessments of personal fitness and the kind of ambitions our respondents had to improve their current levels of fitness. We were interested to see if there was a connexion between what our respondents did which could make them fit (or fitter) and how they saw themselves. When our data was assembled, it would appear that, however high any of the groups, male or female, assessed their current levels of fitness, they all wanted to be fitter than they were.

It also suggested that there was no necessary connexion between what the respondents did and the levels of fitness they assessed themselves to be at, as distinct from the correlation between participation and the desire for fitness. Bangladeshi females, for example, though mentioning sport as less than 10 per cent of their total leisure activities, reckoned themselves to be fitter than Caribbean or Chinese females for whom sport represented a quarter of their leisure. Much the same could be said of other ethnic groups, male and female. Some of the most active groups assessed themselves relatively low in fitness.

With one exception (African), more females than males in all ethnic groups said they wanted to be fitter than they were though the differences between the genders were very small.

The recorded interviews threw into sharp relief the differences between males and females in their perceptions of what constituted 'free time' in which they could follow their own inclinations. South Asian females, in particular, seemed to have less time that they could call their own and were under greater constraints in their use of it. All females undertook a range of social, family and domestic responsibilities which males seemed to play little part in. Females saw fitness as a primary objective in taking part in games or other physical activities but this was often associated with improvements to their self-image. They also saw their activities as an integral part of their social life.

Males, on the other hand, played the game for the sake of the game and saw fitness as a bonus. Only two interviewees referred to its social aspect and it was clear that, for them, the social element came after, and was actually quite distinct from, the activity itself.

The School Experience

It would have been interesting and valuable to have included a substantial section within the questionnaire on the school experience of the respondents and in particular on their participation in PE and games whilst they were pupils. In this way, a direct comparison between their involvement then and after school would have been possible. However, it was believed at the time of drafting the questionnaire — and subsequent experience showed it to be correct — that it was already very demanding and to increase its size yet further would place unreasonable demands on both the field researchers and the respondents.

Instead, it was decided to include the school experience as a major area within the interview schedule. Although the numbers of respondents interviewed made numerical analysis of their observations of little value, the insights that they provided were of real value, especially when set against the quantitative data from the questionnaire which forms the basis for the remainder of this section.

There were wide variations in the level of interest shown by parents in their children's educational experience. All the white interviewees reported that their parents took an interest in their education and gave practical support when and how they could. The extent to which they were able to do this varied according to their educational experience. At the one extreme within the white interviewees was this:

Interviewer: Did you get much help and encouragement from your parents?
Interviewee: Certainly, yes. I had a great deal of support from my parents when I was at school. They helped with homework most nights — that sort of thing; lots of encouragement. My mother spent evenings helping me, testing me when, you know, there was a French test, working with me, even though she'd never done it herself. She put a lot of time in.

Another interviewee explained that she used to talk a lot with her parents when she was still at primary school but that it got less as she grew older.

Maybe because they had both left school at fourteen so they couldn't relate what I was doing to what they had done. They were interested but didn't really know what was going on.

Parents of interviewees from the ethnic minority groups had particular problems since their school experience had usually been quite different from their children's. An Indian female expressed it well and what she said was echoed by respondents from all the minority groups.

Well, because of their educational background, because they were educated in India, in India [it was different from] what the system was like here so they didn't really take that much interest. But having said that, they were always for, you know 'You must do well.' But they couldn't help so much really because they didn't have the knowledge of what the system was like here. I mean, even down to simple things like exams. They weren't always aware of how much revision you had to do, how much time your revision had to take to gear you towards passing an exam. And it's mainly at times like that, that I felt they really didn't understand so much.

We would like to emphasize, however, that although this problem was common to all minority groups, it was not universal. There were some members in all ethnic groups who were fortunate in having parents who were willing and able to take an informed interest in their children's education.

It was clear from interviewees that however much interest parents might show in their children's education, their performance in physical education was given a lower priority by the majority of them. This was true of all ethnic groups. Even those parents whom the interviewees reported as showing a keen general interest in their progress at school were less concerned about what they were doing in PE. The white British interviewee quoted above said in response to a question on her parents' interest:

> No. I used to do keep fit with my mother. She used to watch [inaudible] on TV and she did some exercises to keep fit and when we were children we joined in with her . . . She was about thirty-five and she was putting on weight and so she did exercises. But not as a subject, that was never so important.

There were exceptions, like the interviewee whose mother had been a PE teacher and another whose father was interested:

> **Interviewer:** Were they interested in what you did in PE?
> **Interviewee:** Yes, they generally asked what we'd done and whether we enjoyed it.
> **Interviewer:** Did they think it was as important as other lessons?
> **Interviewee:** I don't think my mum did as much but I think my dad used to think it was as important as the other things.

Most of the interviewees who were of Indian, Pakistani and Bengali origin said that their parents were uninterested in their PE lessons. Some put it down to the same reason as for their more general lack of interest — lack of knowledge of what it was all about at school. Others suggested that they did not take it as a serious subject. As one Pakistani male put it:

> I think they thought it was a waste of time. That time could be better spent in learning something that would be more useful in life.

However, this was not always the case. A Bengali female said of her parents:

> They encouraged us a lot. All three of us represented the school. More in the education side, but obviously, because we enjoyed sports they backed us up as much as they could.

There was, perhaps, a suggestion that of all the ethnic groups, parents of the Caribbean group showed a greater interest in PE. One male spoke of his mother's encouragement:

Like, one time I was chosen to be on the [school] football team and I didn't have a pair of boots and on the day of the first match my mum took me out shopping and bought those boots. We got back just in time for me to play in the game.

Another thought back to her experience at primary school:

Like, when I wanted to do gymnastics, she encouraged me to do that. She paid for me to go to a special school after school was finished. That was in primary school. But when I got to secondary school they didn't do anything like that, so I lost interest.

It was, however, inconclusive. There were, as we have indicated, variations across ethnic groups: some parents showing an interest and supporting their children in PE, most of them not.

It is more pleasant to be able to record that, although most of the interviewees themselves did not think that PE was 'important' in the way that academic lessons were, they were almost unanimous in saying that they enjoyed it. Males and females in all ethnic groups said it with more or less enthusiasm. Most had favourite activities which they particularly enjoyed and others which they did not, but on balance it was recalled as an enjoyable part of the curriculum. Even the interviewee who recollected all sorts of problems about being associated with people she instinctively didn't want to be like had this to say:

I enjoyed PE but I never wanted to be on the hockey team or the lacrosse team. I had a prejudiced attitude against people [members of staff] who took games . . . They were hearty and butch, in a girls school. And lacrosse I thought was a stupid game, and, yes, there was a sense that sporty girls were not very cool. It was an attitude problem when I was there. They were all big and muscley and strong and we were all smoking you know. And worried about hair-styles and clothes. It seemed to be like two cultures.

More typical was the recollection of this Indian female:

I love PE. I didn't sort of take it seriously, I don't know why, but I was getting in there and getting involved. I enjoyed being with the other girls in the class.

Though another one who enjoyed it just as much, recalled that the liking was not universal. She then went on to regret the waste of talent among Asian girls at her school:

A lot of girls in my class hated sports. They'd do anything to get out of it you know; forge their parents signatures; write letters — a lot of English girls as well. I think there were more Asian girls there who enjoyed it more than the English girls. I think it was probably because they weren't allowed out after school, or whatever. Making use of what they'd got really. A lot of the girls — Asians — did rather well, I thought. But it's a pity that that talent was wasted — not allowed to be shown anywhere else. It should be, really.

Sports and Games Played

Respondents were asked to list any activities they were currently taking part in. The results are contained in Tables 9(a) and 9(b) and give the number of times each activity was cited by members of each ethnic group and for males and females separately.

Each of the two tables starts by recording the number and proportion of each ethnic group who took part in no activity at all. The gender difference across the whole sample was marked: 72 (15.2 per cent) of males but 143 (28.2 per cent) of females were inactive. The inactive males fell neatly into two groups. Between a fifth and a quarter of all Bangladeshi, African, East African Asian and Pakistani males were inactive and formed the first, whilst Chinese (8.5 per cent), Indian (7.2 per cent) and white British (11.5 per cent) formed the second. Inactive females fell into no such neat division. The greatest proportion of inactive females were found in the Bangladeshi group (48.9 per cent), next came the Pakistanis (46.5 per cent), the Africans (42.9 per cent) and the Indians (33.9 per cent). Even the Caribbean females were found to have almost a quarter (23.4 per cent) who were inactive, whilst there were 16.4 per cent of white British and 9.9 per cent of Chinese who said they were taking no part in active recreation.

Among the males, the most popular activities were football (154), badminton (129), snooker (108), swimming (102) and pool (84). Among females the most popular activities were swimming (145), badminton (133), keep fit (81), dancing (61) and aerobics (59).

Substantial inter-ethnic variations in the proportions of those active in sport among males were relatively rare. It is notable that 60 per cent of Bangladeshis play football, for example, more than 10 per cent more than white British, 15 per cent more than Pakistanis and 25 per cent more than Caribbeans. Conversely, fewer Bangladeshis go swimming than any other of the major ethnic groups. In badminton, a massive 63.8 per cent of active Chinese respondents took part, followed at some distance by Indians (42.4 per cent) and Bangladeshis (42.2 per cent). However, there were no examples of substantial involvement in an activity by only one ethnic group (with the exception of Carramboard by the Bangladeshis). Of the most popular activities, only football was an outdoor team game; the remainder were indoor, individual. Five of the six most popular activities were competitive. It is perhaps worth noting that pool and snooker — two of the most popular activities among males, fifth and third respectively in overall rank order — whilst they are certainly games of skill, do not promote physical fitness in the way that most of the other activities do. If they were taken out of the

Table 9(a): Games Played by Ethnic Origin and Gender: Males

Activities	Bang	Afr	Caribb	Chin	EAA	Ind	Pak	W/Brit	Totals
No activities	15	5	11	6	4	7	13	11	72
%	24.6	20.0	25.0	8.5	25.0	7.2	24.5	11.5	15.2
Carramboard	14	–	–	–	1	2	2	–	19
Gulli Danda	–	–	1	1	–	–	1	–	3
Kabbadi	–	–	–	–	–	1	–	–	1
Badminton	19	–	10	37	5	36	8	14	129
%	42.2	–	31.3	63.8	41.7	42.2	21.6	16.9	34.7
Basketball	1	–	10	5	–	6	1	1	24
Boxing	1	1	2	1	–	2	2	2	11
Fencing	–	–	–	1	–	–	–	–	1
5 x Football	11	–	9	8	4	21	4	14	71
Gymnastics	–	–	–	1	–	–	–	–	1
Ice hockey	–	–	–	1	–	–	–	–	1
Ice skating	–	1	–	2	–	1	–	1	5
Judo	–	–	1	–	–	–	–	2	3
Karate	1	–	–	1	–	4	2	1	9
Martial arts	–	1	2	9	1	3	4	4	24
Roller hockey	–	–	–	1	–	–	–	–	1
Roller skating	–	–	–	–	–	1	2	–	3
Squash	2	1	2	6	3	16	5	12	47
Table tennis	3	1	8	18	2	18	10	4	64
Ten-pin bowling	–	2	1	7	–	3	1	5	19
Trampolining	–	–	–	1	–	1	–	–	2
Volleyball	3	–	2	3	–	3	–	1	12
Weightlifting	7	2	2	1	1	2	1	3	19
Weight training	3	8	7	6	–	16	10	15	65
Billiards	2	–	1	1	–	1	1	–	6
Darts	–	1	–	1	1	7	1	4	15
Pool	12	5	12	5	3	29	4	15	84
%	26.7	26.3	37.5	8.6	25.0	34.1	10.8	18.1	22.6
Snooker	8	2	8	19	1	35	14	21	108
%	17.8	10.5	25.0	32.8	8.3	41.6	37.8	25.3	29.1
Aerobics	2	1	1	–	1	1	–	3	9
Dancing	3	3	2	1	–	5	1	1	16
Keep fit	1	1	2	–	–	5	3	2	14
Yoga	1	–	–	–	–	1	–	–	2
Life saving	–	–	–	–	–	–	–	2	2
Swimming	6	4	11	18	–	19	10	39	102
%	13.3	21.0	34.4	31.0	–	20.7	27.0	47.0	27.5
Archery	–	1	–	–	–	–	–	–	1
Athletics	1	–	–	3	–	1	–	1	6
Bowls	–	–	–	1	–	–	1	2	4
Curling	–	–	–	–	–	1	–	–	1
Cycling	2	8	2	9	3	3	1	7	35
Fishing	–	–	–	1	–	1	–	3	5
Golf	–	–	–	–	–	4	–	10	14
Horse riding	–	–	1	–	–	2	1	1	5
Jogging	1	1	2	10	1	2	–	3	20
Karting	–	–	–	–	–	–	–	1	1
Motor cycling	–	–	–	–	–	–	–	1	1
Motor racing	–	–	–	–	–	1	–	1	2
Running	2	–	2	3	–	3	1	6	17
Tennis	3	1	2	10	5	8	4	10	42
American football	–	1	1	2	–	–	–	–	4
Baseball	–	–	–	–	–	–	–	1	1

Table 9(a)   (Continued)

Activities	Bang	Afr	Caribb	Chin	EAA	Ind	Pak	W/Brit	Totals
Cricket	2	–	4	7	4	18	12	8	55
Football	27	5	11	20	5	31	16	39	154
%	60.0	26.3	34.4	34.5	41.7	36.5	43.2	47.0	41.5
Hockey	–	–	1	2	2	2	–	–	7
Lacrosse	–	1	–	1	–	–	1	–	3
Netball	–	1	–	–	–	–	–	–	1
Rugby league	–	–	–	2	1	–	–	1	4
Rugby union	–	1	–	1	–	–	1	–	3
Softball	–	–	–	2	–	–	–	–	2
Canoeing	–	–	–	–	–	1	–	1	2
Sailing	–	1	–	1	–	–	–	–	2
Sub-aqua diving	–	–	–	–	–	–	–	1	1
Water skiing	–	–	–	1	–	–	–	–	1
Windsurfing	–	2	–	–	–	–	–	3	5
Ballooning	–	–	–	–	–	–	–	1	1
Camping	–	–	1	3	–	1	–	6	11
Climbing	2	–	–	–	–	–	–	1	3
Gliding	–	–	–	–	–	–	1	–	1
Mountaineering	–	1	–	–	–	–	–	–	1
Parachuting	–	1	–	–	–	–	1	–	2
Rambling	–	–	1	2	–	1	–	5	9
Shooting	–	–	1	1	–	1	1	–	4
Skiing	–	–	–	1	–	1	–	4	6
Thai Boxing	–	–	–	–	–	–	–	1	1

The percentages included for individual activities represent the proportion of active respondents in each ethnic group citing that activity.

reckoning, they would be replaced by weight training and table tennis which are clearly much more minority activities. In this they may be compared with the female respondents whose top-ranking activities were all much more conducive to fitness.

For participating women, swimming was proportionally the first or second most popular activity in all the ethnic groups. However, the rates of participation do show marked differences between the ethnic groups. For example, 56.8 per cent of active white British women cite swimming as one of their activities; nearly 50 per cent of Chinese, Indian and Pakistani respondents swam but only 22.7 per cent of Bangladeshis do so. Badminton is clearly favourite with Bangladeshis, with over half saying that they participate — a proportion only exceeded by Chinese (68.4 per cent) and Pakistanis (66.7 per cent). Keep fit was most popular with Pakistanis (41.6 per cent) and Caribbeans (38.6 per cent), but had little attraction for Bangladeshis (9.1 per cent). Caribbeans (31.8 per cent) were most attracted to dancing, with Africans second (25.0 per cent) and the remaining groups around 18 per cent. In other sports, Indians (27.8 per cent) and Bangladeshis (13.6 per cent) were notably more active in tennis. Overall, the Chinese females were clearly the most active group — the only one to have significant numbers of ice skaters and ten-pin bowlers. All the most popular activities were indoor, individual and, with the exception of tennis, non-competitive.

Table 9(b): Games Played by Ethnic Origin and Gender: Females

Activities	Bang	Afr	Caribb	Chin	EAA	Ind	Pak	W/Brit	Totals
No activities	22	9	18	7	1	19	47	18	143
%	48.9	42.9	23.4	9.9	12.5	33.9	46.5	16.4	28.8
Carramboard	9	–	–	–	–	1	7	1	18
Gulli Danda	–	–	–	–	–	1	1	1	3
Badminton	12	4	15	39	2	18	24	19	133
%	54.5	33.3	26.3	68.4	50.0	50.0	66.7	21.6	40.9
Basketball	2	2	1	2	–	1	2	4	14
5 x Football	1	2	–	1	–	–	1	1	6
Gymnastics	–	–	–	2	–	1	–	–	3
Ice skating	–	–	–	10	1	4	3	5	23
Judo	–	–	–	–	–	–	–	1	1
Karate	–	–	1	2	–	–	–	3	6
Martial arts	–	–	–	2	–	–	1	2	5
Roller hockey	1	–	–	–	–	–	–	–	1
Roller stating	–	2	1	3	–	–	1	6	13
Squash	–	–	2	8	1	5	2	9	27
Table tennis	2	–	3	4	1	3	4	2	19
Ten-pin bowling	–	–	1	12	–	–	–	8	21
Trampolining	–	–	3	4	–	–	–	–	7
Volleyball	3	1	2	5	–	3	2	–	16
Weightlifting	–	2	1	–	1	–	1	2	7
Weight training	–	1	3	2	–	1	2	13	22
Darts	–	–	–	–	–	1	1	3	5
Pool	–	2	8	11	1	2	3	8	35
Snooker	–	–	3	4	–	3	4	3	17
Aerobics	2	4	13	10	2	4	5	19	59
%	9.1	33.3	22.8	17.5	50.0	11.1	13.9	21.6	18.2
Break dancing	3	–	–	1	–	–	–	2	6
Dancing	4	3	18	10	4	–	7	15	61
%	18.2	25.0	31.8	17.5	100.0	–	19.4	17.0	18.8
Keep fit	2	4	22	7	2	7	15	22	81
%	9.1	33.3	38.6	12.3	50.0	19.4	41.6	25.0	24.9
Popmobility	–	–	5	3	–	–	–	6	14
Yoga	–	1	2	2	3	2	4	2	16
Life saving	–	–	–	–	–	–	–	2	2
Swimming	5	4	20	27	4	18	17	50	145
%	22.7	33.3	35.1	47.4	100.0	50.0	47.2	56.8	44.6
Archery	–	–	–	1	–	–	–	–	1
Athletics	2	–	2		–	–	–	–	4
Bowls	–	–	–	–	–	–	–	3	3
Cycling	2	–	4	6	–	2	5	17	36
Golf	–	–	–	–	–	–	–	2	2
Horse riding	–	–	1	–	–	–	2	5	8
Jogging	2	1	–	1	–	2	1	8	15
Running	–	1	2	1	–	–	–	4	8
Tennis	3	–	3	6	–	10	5	6	33
Triathlon	–	–	–	–	–	–	–	1	1
Baseball	–	–	–	1	–	–	–	–	1
Cricket	–	–	–	–	–	1	–	1	2
Football	–	–	1	–	–	3	–	4	8
Hockey	–	–	1	1	–	2	2	2	8
Lacrosse	1	–	–	–	–	–	–	–	1
Netball	1	–	4	7	–	5	5	2	24
Rounders	1	2	–	9	–	2	1	2	17
Softball	–	–	–	1	–	–	–	–	1

Table 9(b) (Continued)

Activities	Bang	Afr	Caribb	Chin	EAA	Ind	Pak	W/Brit	Totals
Canoeing	–	–	–	–	–	1	2	1	4
Rowing	–	–	–	–	–	1	1	–	2
Sailing	–	–	–	–	–	1	–	1	2
Sub-aqua diving	–	–	–	–	–	–	1	2	3
Water skiing	–	–	–	1	–	–	–	1	2
Windsurfing	1	–	–	–	–	–	–	2	3
Bobsleigh	–	–	–	1	–	–	–	–	1
Camping	–	1	2	1	–	1	1	9	15
Climbing	–	–	–	–	–	–	–	2	2
Mountaineering	–	–	–	1	–	–	–	–	1
Orienteering	–	–	–	2	–	–	–	–	2
Rambling	2	1	4	2	4	2	4	11	28
Shooting	–	–	–	–	–	–	–	1	1
Skiing	–	–	1	–	1	–	–	1	3
Abseiling	–	–	–	–	–	–	–	2	2

The percentages included for individual activities represent the proportion of active respondents in each ethnic group citing that activity.

However, all these data must be seen in the context of the very substantial numbers of females who did nothing at all. Thus keep fit may be the third most popular activity among those who participated (24.9 per cent) but it actually involved a smaller proportion of all females than fell into the totally inactive group (28.8 per cent). In this group, Bangladeshis (48.9 per cent) and Pakistanis (46.5 per cent) were prominent.

It is interesting to compare the current activities revealed by the questionnaire data with the comments made by interviewees on their experience of games and PE at school. As noted earlier, all except one of those interviewed said that they generally enjoyed PE at school. They were asked which of the activities did they enjoy. For females, the most popular were netball, rounders, tennis and swimming. For males it was football, badminton, swimming and basketball. Again the gender divide was the significant feature: the majority of the games remembered with pleasure by the males were team games whereas the females spoke more of individual activities.

Again, few males spoke of positively disliking many activities and for those who did so it was usually a case of not being very good at it, for example:

> Well I didn't really enjoy football, but I played it. I never could get the skills together; the tackling and the dribbling, and I couldn't compose myself enough to shoot at goal!

This interviewee — a Caribbean male — was in any case a member of the school's athletics team and would have preferred to train for that.

Females recalled with much more feeling the activities they really disliked and of these, cross-country running was top of the list. Even the most active of the interviewees said of it,

Oh, they did cross-country in the winter. That was a bit of a bind when it was snowing and you had to go out. Cross-country, I didn't like that much!

Other comments included,

Cross-country! We all had to go on cross-country. Everyone had to go and I *hated* it.

and,

We sometimes went cross-country running. I hated that because I used to get wet through in the rain.

Hockey was next on the list of least favourite games and the sort of recollections expressed by those who disliked it might be summarized by this Caribbean interviewee:

Hockey I really didn't like. That's the one I can remember. Getting hit in your shins with a hockey stick: the mud! Playing in the mud! Oh, I don't know; I just think it's a horrible game.

For one of our interviewees, a Chinese female now active in a range of games, PE at school was heartily disliked because it was compulsory and because all the emphasis was on the high achievers.

In my free time now I do a lot more sports than I ever did at school . . . If you were the most talented person you were the only person that was encouraged. But mainly they put you all in a group and made you do the same things, whether you liked it or not. So it just got, well, so I hated it then.

She was, however, very much the exception. We would emphasize that our overriding impression from listening to the interviews and reading the transcripts was the enjoyment evident in the interviewees' voices when they recalled the games and other activities they took part in at school. This enjoyment was equally present both for those who had kept up their participation since leaving school and for those who, for whatever reasons, had not. This was true too, for those groups already identified as low participants in sport and physical recreation — Pakistani and Bangladeshi females.

The Impact of Ethnicity and Religion on Participation

We wanted to reveal and examine any differences in participation in sport and recreation between the ethnic and religious groups and to do this we adopted a number of indices of participation. This made it possible to comment on types of activity rather than attempt to deal with very large numbers of individual ones. The first of these was a general participation index and the remainder were frequency counts of the number of times various types of activity were mentioned. It is possible to devise a number of different types of classification of activities, but the following were thought to be appropriate for our purposes:

Team contact sports — (e.g. hockey, football)
Team non-contact sports — (e.g. volley ball)
Individual contact sports — (e.g. judo)
Individual non-contact sports — (e.g. badminton, aerobics)
Water sports — (e.g. swimming)
Countryside sports — (e.g. walking)
Indoor sports — (which will include any of the above)
Outdoor sports

A general index of participation is very hard to establish for a number of reasons. Although one can — and we did — ask questions about type of activity and frequency, the nature of our data made it difficult to distinguish, in terms of overall participation, between someone who took part in only one activity but did so every day — e.g. an enthusiastic judo competitor — and someone who took part in six different activities per week, but only at a low level of involvement, effort and commitment. Nevertheless a general index was felt to be potentially useful, and so a four-point scale was devised ranging from active participant, moderate participant, occasional participant, to non-participant. This was based on a summation of responses which were then classified, and while far from perfect, it appears to have been at least satisfactory. We defined each category as follows:

Active participant (Two activities per week or more)
Moderate participant (One activity per week, or several less frequently)
Occasional participant (Activity mentioned in some way)
Non-participant

These indices produced data suitable for a series of two-way analyses of variance which enabled differences between ethnic groups, religious groups, the genders etc. to be examined in terms of the various participation indices.

Ethnicity and General Participation

Analysis confirmed what has been shown elsewhere, namely that males participate in physical activities more than females, with the average rating for each male ethnic group clustering round the moderate category. This was to be expected.

Females, on the other hand, show a greater range of mean scores from moderate to occasional. The East African Asian group, which was very small, completely reverses the trend, but the size of the group ruled out any meaningful conclusions. These differences between the genders are statistically significant ($P<.01$) i.e. we would be unlikely to get such results just by chance.

Looking at the ethnic groups themselves, the Chinese and white British show the highest levels of participation and the Bangladeshi and Pakistani the lowest. Differences between the highest (Chinese) and two lowest participation groups (Bangladeshi and Pakistani) were again statistically significant ($P<.01$). Of equal interest is the significant interaction effect which is shown by the fact that the difference between male and female participation mean scores is much greater for Bangladeshi, Pakistanis, African and Indian groups than it is for Caribbean, white British and Chinese. Thus it would seem that some combinations of ethnicity and gender have a much greater effect on general participation than others. The variation between males across the ethnic groups is quite slight. On the other hand, to be female and either Bangladeshi, Pakistani and possibly African, would appear to accentuate the difference in overall participation as compared to men than would be the case for being female and Chinese or white British. The policy implications of these data are self-evident.

Religion and General Participation

Muslims, Hindus and Sikhs participated less than Christians or those of no belief. The only statistically significant differences were between Muslims and Christians, and between Muslims and those of no belief. The number of Buddhists was very small.

Again, religion and gender combined to affect participation. This showed up in the much greater difference in participation between the genders among Muslims, Hindus, Sikhs and Buddhists than was found between the genders among Christians and those professing no religious belief. It seemed an inescapable conclusion that religious/cultural factors can powerfully affect the freedom of females to participate.

Classification of Activities

Participation in sport or physical activity can occur in a host of ways as the list in Tables 9(a) and 9(b) testifies. For practical purposes, it was necessary to group activities into the more manageable number of categories already described. Individuals were 'scored' according to the number of times they mentioned a particular type of activity so that means and variances could be calculated for ethnic groups, genders, religious groups, etc. Although this sub-division of activity meant that mean scores in any one classification were inevitably low — sometimes near zero — the data analysis produced interesting and meaningful results. It is suggested that it was not the absolute average score given to any group which was of real interest but rather how that average compared with the averages of other groups, and also how averages varied with different types of classification of sport.

Outdoor activities.

In an area of the country which is well known for its wide participation in such sports as association football, rugby union, rugby league and hockey, it was not surprising that male involvement in some form of outdoor sport was well represented. We report elsewhere that soccer, including the 5-a-side form, was the most popular male activity. Our analysis confirmed this, and also showed how females participated less than males in every ethnic and religious group. It might have been expected that both male and female white British would be most involved in outdoor sports since these are part of their heritage. This was indeed the case with statistically significant differences between them and Bangladeshis, Caribbeans and Pakistanis ($P<.01$ in each case).

The same pattern appeared with religious groups, although there was no significant difference between the groups, leading to the conclusion that cultural rather than religious influences were operative here.

Indoor activities.

Here it was immediately obvious that a different pattern obtained. On average women took part just as much as men (means 1.02 and 1.04 respectively) but this concealed the fact that among the Chinese and white British (also among Buddhist and Christian), women took part more than men; while among Bangladeshis and Indian (and among Sikhs and Hindus) the pattern of men taking part more than women still applied. In other words, ethnicity and gender combined to affect participation in indoor activities. Being female and Chinese or white British increased the likelihood of taking part, but being female and Indian or Bangladeshi decreased it. Similar results were found with regard to religion where being Buddhist or Christian and female increased participation, while being Hindu and to a lesser extent Sikh, decreased it. The significance of these findings for policy formulation is, we would suggest, considerable.

There were also differences between the ethnic groups, with Chinese being involved in significantly more indoor sports than Bangladeshis and Pakistanis ($P<.01$) — and almost significantly more than Africans. Between the religious groups Hindus were significantly more active than Muslims or Sikhs ($P<.01$) and Christians more than Muslim ($P<.01$, and Sikhs, $P<.05$).

The data thus confirm what might have been expected from common observation, namely that men take part in more activities outdoors than women, but that indoors there is little difference between them. The high participation in football by men, and in badminton, swimming and keep fit by women account in large part for this. However, the combined effects of gender and ethnic group, and gender and religion reveal patterns within these generalities.

Team activities.
Whether one looked at team activities in terms of contact sports (e.g. soccer, hockey, in which individuals frequently make physical contact with opponents), or as non-contact sports (e.g. volleyball where they are physically separated by the net) the same picture emerged. Both genders in all ethnic groups and religions took part, but with the men significantly more involved than females. It was hardly surprising that team contact sports were mentioned more than non-contact sports, simply because there are so many more of them. Nor was it any cause for surprise that so few females took part in them. However, female involvement in non-contact team games was also very small. Their involvement in games such as volleyball was very low. No differences in terms of participation were found between either ethnic or religious groups, and gender did not combine with ethnicity or religion to affect participation.

Individual activities.
Participation in sports such as the martial arts, boxing, wrestling and self-defence was extremely low. Even where an exaggerated vertical scale was used, the participation for women was virtually nil apart from that of a few Chinese and white British. There was a significant difference between the genders, but this was largely a case of a few men taking part, compared with almost no women at all. With such low responses it was not surprising that there were no significant differences between either ethnic or religious groups.

When it came to individual, non-contact sports, however, a picture very similar to that for indoor activities is presented. This is logical since badminton and swimming were well reported by both genders, and other indoor, non-contact activities such as keep fit and dancing, were mentioned frequently by women. The mean scores for men and women are slightly higher than those for indoor activities, indicating that this classification must also include a number of outdoor sports and activities, but as with indoor activities, there was no significant difference between the genders.

Chinese participation was significantly greater than Bangladeshi and Pakistani ($P<.01$ in both cases); white British participation was greater than Pakistani ($P<.01$) and Bangladeshi ($P<.05$) and Indian was also significantly greater than Pakistani ($P<.05$). Among the religious groups Hindus and Christians were more involved than Muslims, ($P<.01$ in each case).

Significant interactions (ethnic groups and religion combining with gender) were also recorded. These show that whereas for Chinese, white British and Caribbeans the female participation is slightly higher than the males, for Africans, Bangladeshis, Indians and Pakistanis the females participate less than the males. Buddhist, Hindus and Sikhs showed much less participation among women, whereas Christians, those with no belief and perhaps a little surprisingly Muslims all showed little difference between the genders.

Water sports.
Although this category could include a wide variety of activities, both indoor and outdoors, in fact it should be predominantly interpreted here as swimming, since

that was by far the most frequently cited. It was not expected that responses such as water skiing or dinghy sailing would receive much endorsement from these samples for economic reasons, and this indeed was the case.

The pattern of responses was similar to indoor activities and individual non-contact activities, into both of which, of course, swimming fits. It is notable that the average participation rate for women exceeded that for men in all groups except for Africans and Sikhs. This remained true for Bangladeshis and Pakistanis, and therefore for Muslims, even though their actual participation was very low indeed. There may not have been a great difference between the average participation rates for men and women, but the difference was nevertheless statistically significant. This clear evidence of the popularity of swimming among women in terms of actual participation (as well as the evidence of unfulfilled desires for it demonstrated elsewhere in this section) is again important in terms of policymaking.

The significant difference between the ethnic groups was due to the fact that the white British participated much more than any other group — compared with Bangladeshis and Pakistanis (P<.01) and compared with Caribbeans and Indians (P<.05). There were no significant differences between any other pairs of groups. Among the religious groups Muslims took part significantly less than Christians and those of no belief, (P<.01 in each case). In view of what was said in the chapter on the ethnic minority groups this was hardly surprising.

Countryside activities.
Countryside activities was a category which received an extremely low number of mentions and yet it was important in that women scored higher than men. The category itself is problematic because it can contain a number of diverse activities including walking, climbing, fishing and skiing. Some of these may appeal more to one sex than another and some may also be very expensive either in terms of equipment, travel or both. Fishing is in fact one of the most popular activities for males throughout the UK. In the context of this research, however, differences between groups were to be seen between the white British and both Bangladeshis and Hindus (P<.05 in each case) as well as between the sexes. No differences of any significance were found between religious groups but an interaction effect was noted here, in that whereas Buddhist, Hindu and Muslim women together with those of no belief participated more than men, Christian and Sikh women participated less than men. This could be explained by the sexes taking part in different types of activity within the overall category of countryside activities. It also seems probable that the patterns of response were affected by the nature of the respondents, the great majority of whom were inner-city dwellers.

The Significance of Religion in Participation

It may not be that simply professing allegiance to a religion was an important influence on whether people took part in sport or physical activity, but rather that the importance of religion to the individual is critical. This possibility was explored through re-examining the various categories of participation, and looking to see if the various levels of importance of religion affected all religious groups equally, or whether the influence of some religions was more pervasive in its effect on their believers than others. The examination was carried out separately for the two genders. Differences in participation levels between religious groups have already been discussed. Respondents had been asked if their religion meant a lot to them; had some importance; had not much importance; or had no importance; and these levels of response were used in the analysis. The people (n=218) who professed no belief were obviously excluded from the comparisons, and comments are only made on those categories of activity where some significant statistic was found. It should also be noted that Buddhist (males=5, females=10) were excluded from this analysis on the grounds of sample size, and even the Hindus (males=44, females=27) and Sikhs (males=35, females=18) are relatively small when spread across four levels of religious importance.

For males it did not seem to matter what religion they adhered to, and how important their beliefs were for them as far as general participation in sport was concerned. The pattern for Hindus and Muslims was very similar, and although Christian and Sikh patterns were a mirror image of each other there was no suggestion of a significant interaction. It is interesting to note that when religion was of no importance in day-to-day life — even when professed — the mean participation scores of the four groups were virtually identical.

The responses given by women, however, provided a different pattern. There was a significant difference between the Christians and Muslims (P<.01) and between Christians and Hindus (P<.05) overall. This was noted earlier as the cause of the difference between religious groups when the sexes were combined. But of greater interest was the significant interaction indicated in Hindus and Muslims. For women, it did not appear that the level of importance they gave to their belief in Christianity had any effect on overall participation but for Muslims, and also for Hindus although they were a much smaller group, it seemed that participation tended to rise as the importance of religion decreased. In the light of the earlier description of ethnic, and religious, group characteristics, this was not entirely surprising. It seemed reasonable to speculate that Muslim females who are strongly affected by their belief might well avoid sports as normally practised in Britain because they demand, what for them would be, immodest behaviour.

Outdoor Sports and Religious Importance.
Although no differences were found as far as women were concerned one interesting result emerged from the analysis of male responses, and that was that while for Christians, Hindus and Sikhs there was a general downward trend in participation in outdoor sports as the importance of religion decreased, the reverse was true for Muslims, for whom outdoor sports rose in frequency as the importance of religion diminished. We have been able to arrive at no satisfactory explanation for this phenomenon.

Indoor Sports and Religious Importance.
Earlier comments on indoor sports participation revealed no overall difference in mean scores between males and females, although a significant interaction was seen, and religious group differences were noted. When the genders were considered separately, and the importance of religion taken into account a slightly different picture emerged. For men, it was almost the same as when the sexes were taken together, with the Hindus participating significantly more than Muslims and Sikhs, but also more than Christians (all P<.01). But there were no differences attributable to the importance of religion, and no interaction. More importantly, when men were considered on their own, the Christians were no longer seen to differ from Muslims or Sikhs.

For women, however, the position was different, with the Christians taking part in significantly more outdoor activities than the other groups (P<.01 over Muslims, P<.05 over Sikhs and just below P<.05 over Hindus). On the other hand, like the males, when we looked for differences in participation between those who held their religion to be either 'important', 'fairly important', 'not very important' or 'unimportant', we found no significant differences. This process, of course, included Christians, Hindus, Muslims and Sikhs as well as the less frequently cited religions in each of the 'importance' groups; in the case of females, it concealed an interaction which approached statistical significance.

It is not surprising that the pictures presented by individual non-contact sports for men and women were virtually the same as for indoor activities, because the two categories have so much in common.

Conformity and Participation

Another potential influence on participation was thought to be the extent to which individuals took into account the expected approval of other people, in particular parents, religious teachers, siblings, friends, and their community. A 'Conformity-Independence' scale was therefore devised by combining responses to questions on the importance of such approval, and then re-grouping responses into 'most conforming', 'conforming', 'independent', 'most independent' categories. This new scale was then used in conjunction with ethnic groups, to measure general participation. The sexes were examined separately. No differences were found between the conformity levels for either sex in terms of participation in physical activity. Those who could be described as generally conformist in their views took part in just as much sport as those who were independent of the influence of other people.

When religion was taken into account, however, a different picture appeared as far as the females were concerned. For males, neither religion nor conformity appeared to affect general participation, but for females an interaction effect was noted which almost reached an acceptable level of significance (P<.06).

Table 10(a): Places Games Played by Ethnic Origin and Gender: Males

Ownership of place		Bang	Afr	Caribb	Chin	EAA	Ind	Pak	W/Brit	Totals
Local	(N)	46	14	44	50	9	85	24	107	379
authority	(%)	34.3	17.3	45.4	25.3	27.3	35.1	23.3	46.3	34.7
Sports	(N)	11	5	7	28	13	45	18	23	150
club	(%)	8.2	6.2	7.2	14.1	39.4	18.6	17.5	10.0	13.7
Own	(N)	38	1	1	11	5	16	2	1	75
community	(%)	28.4	1.2	1.0	5.6	15.2	6.6	1.9	0.4	6.9
Religious	(N)	1	1	2	1	–	7	1	2	15
group	(%)	0.7	1.2	2.1	0.5	–	2.9	1.0	0.9	1.4
Education	(N)	8	5	8	61	–	16	20	16	134
	(%)	5.9	6.2	8.2	30.8	–	6.6	19.4	6.9	12.3
Private	(N)	8	17	10	17	1	39	18	47	157
company	(%)	5.9	21.0	10.3	8.6	3.0	16.1	17.5	20.3	14.4
Youth club	(N)	4	2	15	4	2	4	7	1	39
	(%)	2.9	2.5	15.5	2.0	6.1	1.7	6.8	0.4	3.6
Other +	(N)	10	7	7	11	3	21	9	21	89
home	(%)	7.5	8.6	7.2	5.6	3.0	8.7	8.7	9.1	8.2
Don't	(N)	8	1	3	15	–	9	4	13	53
know	(%)	5.9	1.2	3.1	7.6	–	3.7	3.9	5.6	4.8

This suggested that the participation by Muslim females tended to decrease as conformity increased, whereas for Christian females there was a tendency in the opposite direction.

Conformity and participation among females was examined further by splitting the females into three age groups: under 20; 21–25; and over 25. The results did not change the picture radically, but they did show an increase of independence with age. Of those in the youngest group, 57 per cent were rated as either 'independent' or 'most independent' according to the scale used and this increased to 70 per cent for the 21–25 age group and to 77 per cent for the over-25s. For the under-20s, this interaction was significant ($P<.05$) with participation seen to decrease for this female age group among Bangladeshis, Pakistanis and also Caribbeans, whereas the white British and Indians increased their involvement with conformity. Being young and female and either Bangladeshi or Pakistani was associated with a lower participation rate than among other ethnic groups. However, this was not found to be the case with the over-20s where independence increased.

Where Activities Took Place

We wanted to know where their activities were taking place and who was pro-viding the facilities. For each activity, the respondent was asked who was the provider. The results are contained in Tables 10(a) and 10(b). Analysis was made more straightforward by the fact that there was a strong similarity (noted above) across the ethnic groups in terms of games played.

Table 10(b): Places Games Played by Ethnic Origin and Gender: Females

Ownership of place		Bang	Afr	Caribb	Chin	EAA	Ind	Pak	W/Brit	Totals
Local	(N)	10	9	43	33	8	15	29	97	244
authority	(%)	22.7	32.1	38.1	17.8	33.3	17.4	28.2	47.1	32.0
Sports	(N)	6	10	10	29	2	15	13	15	73
club	(%)	13.6	35.7	8.8	15.7	8.3	17.4	12.6	7.3	9.6
Own	(N)	2	1	5	1	–	2	5	2	18
community	(%)	4.5	3.6	4.4	0.5	–	2.3	4.9	0.9	2.4
Religious	(N)	–	–	3	–	–	–	–	2	5
group	(%)	–	–	2.7	–	–	–	–	0.9	0.7
Education	(N)	14	1	8	65	3	10	19	21	141
	(%)	31.8	3.6	7.1	35.1	12.5	11.6	18.4	10.2	18.5
Private	(N)	1	1	16	19	1	2	6	10	56
company	(%)	2.3	3.6	14.2	10.3	4.2	2.3	5.8	4.9	7.3
Youth club	(N)	–	2	9	4	1	1	2	6	25
	(%)	–	7.1	8.0	2.2	4.2	1.2	1.9	2.9	3.3
Other organisation	(N)	9	3	14	12	8	24	25	34	129
and home	(%)	20.5	10.7	12.4	6.5	33.3	27.9	24.3	16.5	16.9
Don't	(N)	2	1	5	22	1	17	4	19	71
know	(%)	4.5	3.6	4.4	11.9	4.2	19.8	3.9	9.2	9.3

For both males (34.7 per cent) and females (32.0 per cent), the major provider was the local authority. If local authority provision and the education service are taken together to arrive at provision by the two major statutory organizations, their importance becomes even more pronounced: males 47.0 per cent and females 50.5 per cent.

For males, the white British (46.3 per cent) and Caribbean (45.4 per cent) groups were most likely to use local authority facilities. African respondents were least likely (17.3 per cent). Other groups hover around the average figure. By comparison with other ethnic groups, Bangladeshis made most use of facilities provided by their own community whilst the part played by religious organizations was negligible. The education service was a major provider for the Chinese (30.8 per cent) but this is clearly a result of the nature of the sample from that group. Pakistanis (19.4 per cent) also relied substantially on education. Africans (21.0 per cent) and white British (20.3 per cent) made substantial use of facilities provided by private organizations and so, to a lesser extent did Indians (16.1 per cent) and Pakistanis (17.5 per cent). Youth clubs were little used except, perhaps, by the Caribbean group (15.5 per cent). Other venues and the home were cited fairly consistently at around the 7.0 per cent mark.

Outside the similarity of provision by the two statutory bodies, the pattern of provision for females varies noticeably from that for males, with the possible exception of the use made by Caribbean females of youth club facilities — like the males, they made more use (8.0 per cent) than any of the other ethnic groups. Little more than half the females cited provision by sports clubs. Whilst Bangladeshi males cited provision by their own community as a substantial item, for females it was a mere 4.5 per cent. Caribbean and Chinese females were the most substantial users of facilities owned by private organizations. The major difference, however, lies in the use of 'other organizations and home.' Females depended on these sources proportionately twice as much as males. Particularly dependent were Bangladeshis (20.5 per cent), East African Asians (33.3 per cent), Indians (27.9 per cent) and Pakistanis (24.3 per cent). It is unfortunate that 'other organizations' and the 'home' were conflated for computer analysis. It is, however, our firm impression, based on inspection of completed questionnaires, that the great majority of entries under this heading referred to the home; probably of the order of four in every five.

Certainly, interview data strongly supported the impression that women commonly used their homes for exercise. For some, it was the only facility they were able to use. A Caribbean female with a young child who was currently inactive for all practical purposes put it this way:

I don't do that [any activities] now, unless I'm in the house and I put on a tape, and I do a bit.
Interviewer: Why did you stop [doing activities elsewhere]?
Interviewee: I feel I just can't be bothered. It's a bit too much. I'm older. *It's too much*! It's too costly to go and do keep fit. How much is keep fit? About a pound. And there's the travel and the baby sitter. I mean, by the end of the day, when you reckon it all up it's too much. Because I can't afford a child-minder — and [the child]'s a bit particular who she goes to . . .

I've got a rower that I used to use, up in my bedroom, and I wanted it to tone me up, but it was giving me muscles instead. I don't want muscles. It was building my body up instead of just toning me up.

Other women cited the additional expense of baby-sitters as a reason for using the home rather than going out. This white British interviewee said:

I do some keep fit on my own at home, when the children have gone to bed. I put the record on and do a bit. Not a lot. But two or three times a week [I do it at home] mainly because I can't afford the baby-sitters so I can go to a proper keep fit class.

But on Monday nights we go to an aerobics class. That's once a week. I would like to go more, but, as I say, you have to pay the baby-sitter.
Interviewer: Have you ever thought of organizing a group?
Interviewee: I have, but you have to go on a course don't you? You have to get — not a diploma — but you have to go on a course . . . but I don't know where you do it.

Others, particularly from the South Asian communities, made use of the home as a place to exercise — in the case of the younger ones, as well as in public places. In a number of cases they had considered forming home-groups for other Asian females. One of the younger Indian respondents said:

I think it's fine [exercise at home]. I mean, I like dancing myself. So long as people enjoy themselves. I picked up some exercises at a keep fit class . . . I used to do about 15 minutes a night in my own bedroom.

I've thought about organizing a group for other ladies but I haven't got round to it. I think the problem will be just getting them out of their houses and getting their parents to let them go. I think they're going to be very iffy about it. They make up some excuse about them being safer inside, or they say she's got something else on . . .

I think that [video/audio tapes specially made for Asian ladies] would help. Because there's no harm in it. I think an older person than me should be in charge, I think there would be no problem . . . I think a video would be a really good idea.

Another young Bangladeshi said of keeping fit:

I do them [exercises] at home. I dance at home because the music is always there when I've got nothing to do. It's something I really enjoy and I can do it whenever I feel like it. I don't have to actually go out to dance classes.
Interviewer: Would AV tapes be useful?
Interviewee: They wouldn't be much use to me but for those Asian ladies that don't go out much — that don't get involved in things much — it would help them.

For others, it was the only opportunity, as one Indian female said of her sister:

She was never into dancing but recently, she has this tape on — God knows what time. I mean, last night for instance, she was up at about eleven o'clock, had the radio on and just doing all this *wild* dancing, and I was trying to get to sleep. Sometimes I'll get up and get involved.

One white British interviewee who included weight training, swimming, aerobics, dance, jogging and running in her current activities, none the less also did keep fit at home.

I've got a full set of videos . . . I do it [at home] because you can do it when you like. It doesn't matter what you look like so much — people seem to get dressed up for an aerobics session — you don't have to

Table 11: Respondents Wishing to Take Part in Activities in Local Authority Facilities But Who Felt Unable to do so by Ethnic Origin and by Gender

		Bang	Afr	Caribb	Chin	EAA	Ind	Pak	W/Brit	Totals
Males	(N)	10	6	6	6	1	15	2	6	52
	(%)	16.4	24.0	13.6	8.5	6.3	15.5	3.8	6.3	11.7
Females	(N)	8	5	20	6	4	9	19	28	99
	(%)	17.8	23.8	26.0	8.5	50.0	16.1	18.8	25.5	21.2

travel. It's just very convenient. And you save money in the long run because usually you have to pay a pound or more to go to an aerobics class . . . I do it mostly on my own but I used to do it with another girl. I used to go round to her house at night every Tuesday . . .

We thought it sensible to ask respondents if they had wanted to take part in activities at facilities run by local authorities but had, for one reason or another, been unable to do so. Numbers responding to this question and its follow-up, 'What might be done to make it more possible?' were small. Clearly, those who took no part in activities and had no ambitions to do so had nothing to say; nor did those who had encountered no problems. This having been said, the number responding (151) was not negligible. It appears that around 20 per cent of the membership of all ethnic groups had experienced some difficulty which prevented them from taking part in an activity (see Table 11). More significantly, whilst 11.7 per cent of males reported a problem, twice as many females (21.7 per cent) did so. Differences between the genders were particularly noticeable in the Pakistani respondents (3.8 per cent of the males but 18.8 per cent of females), and white British (6.3 per cent of males and 25.5 per cent of females.)

For males, the commonest problem was that of feeling that they would be an 'outsider' and for women too, this was of importance. It was voiced most frequently by Indian males. This was followed in importance by 'no time' for males and given some prominence by females. For females the most important reason was lack of single-sex facilities. The majority citing this reason was from Bangladeshi and Pakistani respondents who gave identical responses. Also important for females (and perhaps associated with the issue of single-sex facilities) was the lack of lessons and community disapproval.

As for what might be done to improve matters, the suggestions were not as closely related to the nature of the perceived problems as might be expected. Male respondents thought that the two most effective actions would be to provide more facilities and to provide concessions for the poor and unemployed. For women, it was to provide more facilities and more single-sex facilities, though greater provision of lessons and opportunities for just having fun had a number of supporters.

Although single-sex provision did not form part of the interview schedule, the subject was touched on by two female interviewees. One, a Pakistani female, whose sole activity was aerobics where it was 'all women', was asked if there was anything she would really like to do but felt she could not. She replied with an enthusiasm that was memorable:

> Swimming! I'd *love* to go swimming. [Pause, and then with unmistakable regret] But I can't because there are religious reasons.

Another interviewee, white British, also referred to single-sex sessions and exposed the sort of muddle-headedness that so often defeats good intentions.

> It's funny. One of the things you said [in the questionnaire] about 'Was there any special arrangements made?' I used to go for the swimming on ladies nights at W— Pool. And I thought that was a really good idea for women who didn't really want to go to swim in a mixed pool. Fine! Of course, when you go, they have men attendants. It's against the whole point! I just couldn't see the sense of it.

Local authorities, though by far the leading provider, were not the only ones. We asked our respondents if they had ever applied to join a club or association and been refused. We then asked if they thought they knew the reason for refusal. The numbers responding were very small. The only comment we feel able to make is that, small though the numbers are, it is at least interesting to note that nearly half were of the opinion that racial discrimination was the cause of their exclusion.

Interview material suggested that racial discrimination had affected respondents well before they would normally have started to look for clubs to join, thus ensuring that they did not put themselves into a situation where they would be rejected, either at the time of application or afterwards by white members. A Caribbean male was talking of his experience at school and immediately following leaving.

> At school I used to play with black guys. If you played with the black guys you knew you were going to succeed at something. The white guys, they could be really bad at something but they had one thing over you — they're white. Basically, most of the coaches and people who were putting money into the sport took this into consideration and you'd be sort of left behind. No matter how good you are at school, if your sponsor sees you as something that would, sort of, put his image down, he's not going to go for you.

> In athletics [at school] we were encouraged because we were black and none of the white guys were as fast as us, so we were encouraged. But anything else — football for instance — they were all white guys in the football team. We were sort of scorned from doing that.

One of the Caribbean interviewees had been born in Jamaica and had not come to Britain until he was eighteen years old. He was thus able to compare his experiences before and after migration.

> The Jamaican school system was based roughly on the English school system from the colonial experience. The only difference was that, as a black person, you can aspire to do anything really that you wanted to do, because everyone around you was black. The teacher was black, and even when you went home and watched television, the people on television were black. So you were surrounded by black professionals who inspired you to do anything.

A Pakistani male spoke of his post-school experience:

> My friends play mainly football. They all get together — they're all Asians — and they play with themselves. They usually hire an indoor sports hall and play there.
> **Interviewer**:   Would you really prefer to play with others of your own ethnic group, or would you prefer to play mixed?
> **Interviewee**:   Well, the way I see it is that the white man will not really integrate fully so it doesn't bother me. My friends really want to play with themselves. They just want to play football and relax; get away from everything.

The following is a description of events during a water sports weekend arranged by a white leader for a group of Pakistani males aged between eighteen and twenty. The story was told by the group leader (GL) and one of the members of the group (GM).

> **GL**:   I noticed it when we went to Wales last October for a week-end . . . It was interesting observing this bunch of lads; collectively great. There was in actual fact trouble. It wasn't their fault. There was a sort of holiday camp. A pretty awful place, but there were swimming pools and areas for football and stuff like that: a river where you could take out canoes and so on. And at the top of the camp site there was a bar and night club. Well none of the lads drink, but across from the bar there was this nightclub with a late bar and we got invited. But the collective kind of consciousness was 'Well we oughtn't to go in here because there's going to be trouble.' And as it turned out there was. But I was saying 'Come on! You've got to have a more positive attitude' . . .
> **GM**:   But you could sense from the atmosphere that if we went in there, there's going to be trouble; maybe from the looks we were getting. I don't know. But in the end we said 'All right, we'll go in there and see what happens.'
> **GL**:   What I'm trying to say is that, I got the impression from that

weekend which I never really thought of or experienced before, that Asian and black people in general tend to have a negative expectation when they deal with or approach what's considered white culture. I think it's very unfortunate. There was a fight. As soon as we walk in.

GM: Someone said what are you looking at you black ———. We were just sitting down. We weren't looking at anything. Just listening to the music. Somewhere to go on a Saturday evening. And we got a mouthful.

GL: And needless to say we got thrown out, which I was pretty livid about at the time.

GM: And that same bloke, he started fighting with that old man, didn't he.

GL: The irony of it all was that it was all caused by white people but who gets the blame for it? Our group of people — and I hadn't seen this sort of thing in operation. I'd suspected things like that happened. This is like a microcosm of what goes on all over the place for black people, when they come into contact; when there's more than one or two of them I suppose they're seen as a threat. I don't understand why — well perhaps I do — but to actually see it in operation was a surprise. I mean I've read about the theory — it was an eye-opener for me. So I guess that's another reason why black youngsters are possibly reluctant to get involved in mainstream — like soccer leagues and stuff like that. They'd rather have a quiet life than get that sort of trouble and hassle . . .

For those who did join a local club, the experience could be daunting and the long-term effects on the individual and for race relations could be very unfortunate. A Pakistani who had managed to overcome the sense of rejection that he had felt and had remained in the club, spoke about it and the effects it had had on some of his friends:

Interviewer: You strike me as a very confident, outgoing, friendly young man. There must be a lot of other lads who just haven't got your level of confidence.

Interviewee: You see a lot of the lads who do get a bit of stick if they go and join a football team or whatever. When they get a bit of stick, either they can turn their face or they take it. And a lot of the lads, if they don't want to take it, they come back and then they have that feeling in them, you know; it's that *anger* that it seems they don't let go. And from that point they think bad of English people. They don't tend to mix with anybody. That bad point affects all the other things in their lives.

It can be a matter of little surprise that most Asian and black males said that they preferred to play in teams that were wholly or largely made up from people of their own ethnic origin.

It seemed possible that games playing by other members of the family might have an effect on the probability of respondents being active also. We asked them to say if they had relatives who took part in any of the activities listed. Bangladeshi and African males appeared to have least active members of the family with more than 60 per cent being inactive. Other ethnic groups hovered around the 40 per cent mark. Responses giving one, two, three or four instances of activity within the family were more notable for their similarity across the ethnic groups than any differences.

The most interesting difference was obtained from comparing male and female responses to the question. Female respondents appeared to have many more active persons in their families. The proportion of those who said that no member of the family took part in any activity was almost half that of the male respondents. As a necessary consequence, those members of their families credited with taking part in one or more activities were correspondingly increased. It is possible to speculate at length about this strange difference in the responses between males and females. Again, however, the similarities between the responses given by the different ethnic groups were more striking than any differences.

A major influence on people's aspirations is generally reckoned to be the media. A question seeking to discover the extent to which respondents were influenced by sport shown on TV and in films was included. The commonest response was 'I would like to be able to do that' given by 26.1 per cent of 16–20 year olds, 31.4 per cent of 21–25 year olds and 31.9 per cent of 26–30 year olds. Next most frequent was 'I would like to be like them' (that is, the people taking part) which was given by 13.2 per cent, 18.0 per cent and 10.2 per cent of the same three age groups. Thus, irrespective of age, these two responses accounted for some 40 per cent or more of all responses.

Among the youngest respondents, the Indians (who were, in any case, one of the most active of the ethnic groups) responded most positively to the media, though the Bangladeshis were also prominent among those who 'would like to be able to do that.' Respondents from the middle age band showed a similarity of response which has been one of the most notable features of the study. The most common responses were again to the first two — at a slightly higher level than for the youngest age range. The oldest group repeated the pattern, though here, the least enthusiasm was shown by Pakistani and Bangladeshi respondents. Ethnic groups who had given positive responses in the younger age bands — Indians and Chinese, for example — continued to do so.

Additional light was cast on the effect of the media by the interviews. What seemed to be the case was that those who were already active in a sport tended to watch that sport on TV. They then reported that the sight of people engaged in it on TV encouraged them to go out and try to improve their performance. For example, a Jamaican respondent said:

Yes, definitely. Because to see people do it well gives me some sort of idea that I could do it well, so I go out and try.

A white female respondent, who was very much involved in trying to resuscitate an ailing tennis club, made a similar point but with a real sting in the tail.

> Not me particularly. I'm definitely interested in Wimbledon and I enjoy watching Wimbledon — one of the few tennis tournaments I enjoy watching. And it certainly brings people out to play tennis. You always get a big surge in membership then. I don't really watch much else.

> I think women's sport is terribly neglected on TV.

An Indian female was also a keen Wimbledon watcher:

> Yes definitely. I mean, when Wimbledon was on in the summer; there's Steffi Graff and that. It's a shame I've had no training — not even at school. I never had any knowledge of how to serve or hold the racket, or anything.

A Chinese male who was a squash enthusiast said, in response to the question, 'Has TV encouraged you to play?',

> Yes, very much so. This British Open Squash I was telling you about, they will be showing it on TV this Sunday and I'm looking forward to that programme. TV can help very much in the promotion of sport.

And a Chinese female echoed this view;

> Seeing games on TV doesn't give much motivation. For example, if I disliked cricket I wouldn't go and play it, just because I saw it on the TV. I suppose if you like a game and you see people playing it so well, then you might say 'I must play and I'll do it as well as the people I've seen.' I suppose TV might help that way.

However, those interviewees who were currently inactive or nearly so reported that TV had little effect on them. Thus a Pakistani female:

> I enjoy watching them [people doing activities on TV] but I've never thought of myself doing the same thing. I never followed it up.
> **Interviewer**:   Do you think you might one day?
> **Interviewee**:   I don't think so. Not now.

Unfulfilled Ambitions

It seemed important to discover if there were activities that respondents would like to take part in if they had the chance. The answer to this question is

Table 12:   Unfulfilled Ambitions by Ethnic Origin and Gender

*Ambitions		Bang	Afr	Caribb	Chin	EAA	Ind	Pak	W/Brit
	(M)	27	12	22	40	8	42	17	35
	(%)	44.3	48.0	50.0	56.3	50.0	43.3	32.1	36.5
Yes									
	(F)	19	9	36	47	2	36	53	52
	(F%)	42.2	42.2	46.8	66.2	25.0	64.3	52.5	47.3
	(M)	31	8	17	24	4	48	34	43
	(M%)	50.8	32.0	38.6	33.8	25.0	49.5	64.2	44.8
No									
	(F)	21	9	31	21	6	11	36	38
	(F%)	46.7	42.9	40.3	29.6	75.0	19.6	35.6	34.5

* The percentage figures give the proportion of males and females in each ethnic group who expressed a wish to take part in at least one activity or alternatively said they did not.

contained in Table 12. Whereas males were equally divided between those who would and those who would not, a clear majority (60/40) of females said that there were activities they would like to take part in, given the opportunity. Only Pakistani and white British males deviated from the norm, both groups seeming to have fewer ambitions than the other ethnic groups. Of the female respondents, Chinese and Indians seemed to have most in the way of unfulfilled ambitions and it is interesting to note that these two groups emerged in the analysis of games played as being among the most active.

Exploring this theme further, respondents were asked what activities they would like to take part in and why they did not do so. Their responses were in the form of activities desired and reasons for not taking part. The results are presented in more manageable form by dividing the activities into indoor team games, outdoor team games, indoor individual games and outdoor individual games for males and females separately.

Indoor team activities would seem to have little appeal. Only 25 respondents cited them. Of the reasons given for not taking part, lack of time and expense were most frequent, but perceived lack of or inconvenient facilities and lack of knowledge as to clubs and teams assumed some importance if taken together.

Outdoor team games were cited 37 times with lack of time as the most frequent reason for not taking part. Again, however, lack of or inconvenient facilities taken with lack of knowledge account for a substantial proportion of reasons cited.

Indoor individual games were cited by 98 respondents. Whilst lack of time (26) was mentioned as the commonest reason for not participating, a range of other causes achieved significance. Chief among these was lack of knowledge (22), laziness (15), lack of or inconvenient facilities (11) and lack of friends to go with (11). Outdoor individual activities were mentioned by 194 respondents. Expense was cited by 58, lack of knowledge by 41, lack of or inconvenient facilities by 39 and lack of time by 26.

What seems to be clear is that team games, whether indoor or outdoor, have a relatively low appeal with only 62 citations. Individual activities with 292 citations (30.0 per cent of all respondents) seem to have a much greater appeal. Moreover, this seems to hold for all ethnic groups.

Turning now to the reasons for not taking part, the picture is fairly complex. It is tempting to interpret lack of time as a synonym for laziness or lack of real interest or some other unidentified reason — not least having regard to the occupations of most of the respondents and the very high levels of passive entertainment recorded earlier. Lack of knowledge, however, figures largely as a reason in all types of activity. It is tempting to look for language as a factor in this and certainly it is mentioned by Pakistanis (14 times), Indians (13) and Chinese (17). Bangladeshis gave it as a reason only seven times, however, and it is generally recognized that of all the ethnic minority groups, they and the Chinese are most likely to have language problems. On the other hand, white British respondents gave it as a reason only four times even though they were the largest single group. It may be assumed that it might be the result of a combination of factors of which language might be one but another could be described as general knowledge — the sort of know-how acquired as a result of being actively keyed into the major society.

Expense as a reason for not taking part appeared in relatively small numbers in three of the types of activity but figured prominently in individual outdoor activities. This can largely be accounted for by the types of activity involved. Many of the males mentioned such high-cost activities as motor car and cycle racing, microlight flying and gliding, yachting and the like. Again, the nature of the sample is important. Members of middle-class white society, though unable to afford a yacht or a glider, would be better placed to know someone who had one who needed a crew member and so fulfil their ambition.

Lack of, or inconvenient facilities were a common and substantial theme and this seemed to be a problem for all ethnic groups but with little difference between them once allowance was made for the size of the ethnic groups in the sample.

Overall patterns for females resemble those of males. As with them, so it might be said generally of the females: those groups that were already relatively active were those who showed an interest in doing more. Relatively few cited an interest in team games, either indoor (20) or outdoor (22). What was perhaps unexpected was the preference shown for outdoor individual activities (212) over indoor individual (188). Another marked difference between the genders was that females (although slightly fewer than males in the sample) showed an interest in a wider range of activities. Whilst the males cited individual activities 292 times, females did so 400 times. We can only conclude from this that, whilst they may actually participate less than males, they perhaps have at least as great an interest. We would also note that there was a substantial interest shown in countryside activities — rambling, horse riding, climbing and the like — and that these were frequently cited by South Asian females as desired activities.

The major reason advanced for non-participation was lack of knowledge (112 times). This was the most significant reason for all types of activity except for indoor individual where it came second. As with the males, it seemed less of a problem for the white British group but figured prominently in the Chinese (32), Caribbean (20), Pakistani (18), and Indian (13) groups. The Bangladeshi group cited it only three times but they also showed the lowest level of interest in activities of any of the major groups in the sample. Again, language barriers, whilst they may have some impact, cannot, of themselves, account for the variations between the groups in offering this explanation. As with the males, some other factor is involved though it may, or may not, be the same for both genders.

Next most significant was the lack of or inconvenience of facilities, mentioned 103 times. For the Bangladeshi group this was the major factor in their inability to participate. Although relatively insignificant for the white British group, it was a constant problem for all other ethnic groups and the most significant for those wishing to participate in indoor individual activities. Third overall was lack of time and it may be thought that this could be interpreted as for the male sample.

Lack of single-sex facilities seemed to be a problem only for Pakistanis wanting to take part in indoor individual activities. Similarly, few cited domestic demands as a reason for not doing what they wanted. We found this surprising but concluded that it might be explained by its sheer obviousness.

Expense was an issue that became important for white British females in their desire to take part in outdoor individual pursuits but less of a problem to other ethnic groups. This was in large measure a result of their choices: the expense of some outdoor activities is inherent in their nature — parachuting, hot air ballooning and flying can't be done on the cheap — and generally speaking, the minority groups showed an interest in activities which were not prohibitively expensive.

Summary

In recognition of the length and complexity of the data and comment in this chapter, we attempt to bring out some of the salient issues by posing questions and answering them briefly.

1 Were there any significant differences between ethnic groups in the importance of sport relative to other leisure occupations?
Our findings suggest that there are no differences. Of the ten categories of leisure occupations, sports were the most popular for males as a whole and this held true for six out of eight of the ethnic groups studied. In the two groups for which it was second in popularity (African and white British) it was second by narrow margins.

The major variations were between males and females. Whilst males as a group gave sport as their commonest leisure activity, for females it was third, behind passive entertainments and socializing. Within ethnic groups, Bangladeshi males were four times more likely than females to cite an activity and Pakistani males three times more likely.

2   *Were there any significant differences between ethnic groups in the types of games they played?*

In general terms there were no major differences. When this study began it was suspected that ethnic groups might show preferences for different games and activities. It was thought that white British males, for example, might exhibit a stronger preference for outdoor team games than other groups, or the Caribbean group might take part in more activities than others. None of these preconceptions was justified. The most popular activities for all males were popular for all ethnic groups. Similarly for females, though the activities were different from the males, those which were the most popular with all, were also popular with members of all ethnic groups.

There were, however, substantial variations between ethnic groups in the proportions of those who took part in no activities at all. Although 15.2 per cent of males in the sample were inactive, a quarter of all Bangladeshis, West Indians and Pakistanis took part in no activities. Similarly, although 28.8 per cent of females were inactive, almost half of the Bangladeshi and Pakistani respondents took part in no activities.

The significant differences were not between the ethnic groups but between the genders within ethnic groups. Twice as many Bangladeshi females as males were inactive and the same could be said of the Pakistani group. For the Indian group, males were three times more likely than females to be involved in any activity.

3   *Were there significant variations in the participation rates across the ethnic groups and/or between genders?*

Yes there were. In detail the differences were complex and what follows is simplified to bring out major differences.

Males from all ethnic groups participated more than females (except for East African Asians where the number of respondents was too small to make results reliable). Moreover, the difference in participation levels between the most active group of males — Chinese — and least active — Pakistani — was much smaller than for the most active females — Chinese — and least active — Bangladeshi.

4   *Were there differences in participation rates in different sorts of activities between ethnic groups?*

Yes. For example, Chinese respondents were involved in significantly more indoor activities than Bangladeshis and Pakistanis. These differences were also significantly affected by gender. For example, Chinese and white British females cited more indoor activities than their male counterparts. However, the variations in participation in the categories of activities employed were so complex as to defy simplification here.

5   *Was there evidence of factors other than ethnic difference being responsible for variations in participation?*

Yes. Gender difference was a constant in participation rates. Females usually — though not invariably — recorded lower levels than males. Exceptions were found in water sports (swimming mainly) and countryside activities.

Religion was also a significant factor for females but markedly less so for males for whom it seemed of no consequence so far as participation rates were concerned. For females, a belief in Islam appeared normally to accentuate the gender difference and further depress their participation. It seemed possible that the *importance* attached by respondents to religious beliefs might further affect behaviour and hence, participation, but this was found generally not to be the case.

The results of exploring various constraining factors — the need for approval by parents, religious teachers, siblings and so on — suggested that, however these factors operated, they did not, of themselves, make for significant differences between the ethnic groups in terms of participation. If, however, conformity and religion were taken together, it showed that participation by Muslim women decreased whilst that of Christian women increased. Thus, to be young, female and either Pakistani or Bangladeshi, was to be a member of a low participant group. It is suggested that the evidence supports the view that Islam powerfully reinforces the natural authority of parents and results in the adoption by females of behaviour patterns which reduce participation.

6 Were there any significant variations in the ownership of the places where activities took place?
Perhaps the most significant finding so far as the provision of facilities was concerned was the importance of local authority provision to all ethnic groups. Both for males and females it accounted for about a third of all usage. If the provision owned by the education service was added, the proportion increased to a half. White British and West Indian respondents, male and female, made greatest use of them.

The importance of the home was significantly greater for females generally than for the males. Noteworthy also were the proportions of Pakistani, Bangladeshi, East African Asian and Indian females who used the home. It is plausible to assume that this is a function of belief in Islam. Bangladeshi males were substantially greater users of facilities owned by their community than any other group. Bangladeshi females, on the other hand, made very little use of community facilities. In the light of our comments on the nature of the communities in chapter 3, this came as no great surprise.

Males made greater use than females of facilities provided by commercial suppliers. Among females, the West Indian and Chinese groups made two or three times the use of such facilities than did the others. It must be stressed, however, that the use made by any group was trivial by comparison with local authority-owned facilities.

7 Were there significant variations in the current levels of fitness as perceived by the different ethnic groups, or in the levels of fitness desired?

Male respondents perceived themselves in general as being fitter than females, with Indian males being the most modest in their assessment. Indian females were also the most modest in their assessment among female respondents. This having been said, the similarities were more striking than any differences between the ethnic groups.

There was very little difference between the levels of fitness desired by members of ethnic groups. Most significant was the fact that more than eight out of ten of all respondents said they would like to be fitter than they were.

8   Was there a relationship between perceived levels of fitness, the desire for greater fitness and the activities respondents actually took part in?
There was no correlation between these findings. Indians, males and females, were among the more active of the ethnic groups but gave themselves a low 'fitness rating'. Bangladeshi and Pakistani women were amongst the least active of the groups yet they were keen to be fitter than they were.

9   Was there evidence of overt racism?
Of the small number of respondents in the questionnaire survey who said they had been excluded from a club or association, half said it was, in their view, because of racial discrimination. It might be thought equally significant that substantially larger numbers of respondents said that they did not go to local authority facilities because they felt an 'outsider'. Evidence of racism in many aspects of daily life was abundant in the recorded interviews. We would suggest that this inevitably acted as a constraint on the willingness and ability of people from ethnic minority groups to participate in a range of social activities of which sport was one. Why, after all, should people be expected to put themselves in situations in which they have good reason to suspect they will be rejected?

10   Was there evidence of suppressed desires to be more active in sport and physical recreation?
All ethnic groups, males and females, said there were activities they would like to take part in but could not. Proportionately, more females than males said this. There was little difference between the ethnic groups. Moreover, not only did more females want to take part than males, but they wanted to take part in a significantly greater number of activities. Females and males showed a marked preference for individual, rather than team, activities, and for outdoor rather than indoor. In general terms, those ethnic groups that were already the most active were those who wanted to do more but even the least active (e.g. Bangladeshi and Pakistani females) gave evidence of a desire for greater participation. Countryside activities appeared to offer an attraction to South Asian females. This may have been a consequence of the sample being predominantly urban, but an alternative possibility is that such activities have a less overtly competitive element. Certainly we incline to this view. We suggest that the relationship between physical exercise and competition is essentially a Western European artifact deriving from deeply-held beliefs in the virtues of individualism and personal endeavour. Other

cultures which emphasize the virtues of cooperation for the common good may well be attracted to other forms of exercise with other outcomes. In this connexion we cannot resist the temptation to quote form Gutmann (1978):

> The importance of contests in our society makes it difficult to realize that there are literally thousands of games that are not contests. Japanese kemari, for instance, is a game often called football by Western observers because the ball is kicked by the foot, but the ceremonial object of the game is to keep the ball in the air and the participants are in no sense contestants. Kicking the ball while standing in an area whose four corners are marked out by a willow tree, a cherry tree, a pine tree, and a maple tree, the players act out their sense of universal harmony. No one wins, no one loses. (p. 5)

Chapter 6

The Way Ahead

It seems prudent to consider how far it is right or justifiable to intervene in the lives and common practices of minority groups living in Britain. This issue is most pertinent to the case of South Asian Muslim communities who have settled in Britain though it is not unique to them. The same considerations apply in plural societies, wherever they may be, since pluralism implies equality of access to power and a right to conduct your life within the law, at ease with yourself and without threats from others.

In the brief portraits of ethnic minority groups, we suggested that the great majority of the first generation South Asian settlers were largely from rural backgrounds, with little in the way of formal education and with a poor command of English. The response to their arrival, by successive governments of both persuasions, has been widely seen by those active in research as less than welcoming — Rex and Tomlinson (1979) and Tierney (1982) for instance. In addition, it is a matter of public record that these settlers were subject to discrimination by society at large in all aspects of their daily life. Their corporate, if not individual, strategy in the fact of this was to reconstruct their traditional, complex and varied institutions of family, caste, religion and kinship obligations in an attempt to provide security — physical, moral and social. As we have seen, these institutions have largely survived and have, from time to time, been strengthened by external stimuli such as the publication of Salman Rushdie's *The Satanic Verses*, the Gulf War and at a persistent, though less dramatic level, by the passing of increasingly restrictive legislation regulating the admission of people from the New Commonwealth and Pakistan.

Their children, however, were, and continue to be, inevitably exposed to the impact of British life and thought at their most formative period through their compulsory school experience. Their parents, as those whom we interviewed and others reported by many educational researchers have testified, were, as a result of their limited education and ignorance of the process through which their children were going, unable to take an active part in their education. Though it should be added that they exhibited a touching confidence in the education system.

Moreover, whilst substantial numbers of South Asian parents strove to retain all the values and customs they brought with them, their children's teachers frequently believed that they should work towards their assimilation into British — and essentially middle-class — culture (Troyna and Ball, 1984). The combination of exposure to Western European culture and modes of thought at school and Asian cultures and modes of thought at home had predictable consequences on the youngsters, who had to attempt to accommodate the two very different worlds. Thus for example, Ullah and Brotherton (1989) reported significantly higher levels of anxiety among British Asian adolescents than were found in comparable white British or Afro-Caribbeans. How British-born Asians are coming to terms with this situation has been the subject of studies by Weinreich and Ghuman.

Both come to similar conclusions. Ghuman (1991) was able to compare his findings based on a group in 1987 with a similar group studied in 1974 and found that there was a significant movement towards acculturation. His findings showed that Hindus and Sikhs were more likely to show greater acculturation than Muslims but that the male/female divide was the most significant. Indeed, in a hierarchy which divided males and females and took into account socio-economic status and religion, the least acculturated female group — Muslim females — ranked above the most acculturated males — Hindus and Sikhs. Most significant was the evidence that the females seemed to have retained a belief in and wished to practise a range of traditional 'core' values whilst favouring the adoption of a range of British norms, such as those relating to mixed gatherings, inter-ethnic friendships and the equality of treatment by parents of boys and girls. Equally significant is the fact that of the males, Muslims were most likely to support those views which would retain the traditional role of women.

Weinreich (1990) similarly suggested that 'progressive' young Muslim women (that is, those who were successful in redefining their ethnic identity in their attempts at coming to terms with British society) have identified:

> individualist values to the extent that they wish for greater individual choice and less family surveillance of their behaviour. However, their redefinition of their ethnic identity remains quite distinct from the female version of Anglo-Saxon identity with its strongly individualist orientation . . . They remain with distinctly British Muslim identities. While demonstrating some integration into the wider Anglo-Saxon milieu, their identities have not become assimilated within it. They retain their distinctiveness of ethnic identity intact.

He contrasted their response to the dilemma with those Muslim women who opt for orthodoxy, finding their solution in the adoption of modes of thought and the maintenance of customs and codes of practice of orthodox muslim societies.

Our findings give clear indications that many women would like to take part in a wide range of activities and that they are prevented from doing so. In the case of Muslim women who are of South Asian origin, they suffer from the normal constraints of all female would-be participants — lack of money, the demands of young children, the lack of convenient facilities — but added to these are the additional barriers created, and imposed by men, who transmit and legitimate them by employing the authority of religion, culture and custom.

Unlike America, where the Bill of Rights exerts a substantial influence, and Canada, British law, generally speaking, makes few provisions for ethnic minority communities. In the 1970s, the Union of Muslim Organizations representing bodies in the United Kingdom and Eire, made proposals for consideration by government ministers to introduce legislation for a system of family law to be applied by the courts in cases involving Muslims in Britain. This move achieved nothing. As Poulter (1989) observed, there were a number of difficulties about introducing a separate system. Most cogent of these appeared to be that Muslim family law embodied principles which were contrary to fundamental human rights as set out in treaties such as the European Convention on Human Rights and the International Covenant on Civil and Political Rights. Notable among these were provisions which seemed to discriminate against women. Thus, rules which would permit polygamy, allow the marriage of girls before puberty, ban women from marrying other than Muslim men or enable divorce by *talaq* (the unilateral declaration by the husband) would stand little chance of legislative support. It is now the case that the principle of equality as applied to marriage and family life is firmly established as part of the British legal system and that the state cannot and will not support discrimination against women based on customs arising from 'religious beliefs propounded, interpreted and enforced exclusively by men' (Poulter, 1990).

Ghuman (1991) similarly expressed a view of traditional South Asian family life and the issue of gender and suggests that it is a view covertly shared by many British men.

> Women are often thought to be different from, if not inferior to, men. The traditional role of women is confined to the household activities of child care, housekeeping and being a hostess. This notion is not unlike one held by British men before World War I and some feminists would say that it is cherished now by most men (Greer, 1984).

In this context the comments of the South Asian woman on the gender difference, as manifested by the differences in personal liberties given to, and the expectations parents have of the behaviours of sons and daughters, reported in an earlier chapter, gain a sharp poignancy.

Evidence in chapter 5 clearly indicated that there was a substantial unfulfilled desire on the part of female respondents to take part in a wide range of activities. Our findings and those of others have established that many young women wish to adopt a lifestyle that retains the fundamental beliefs and practices of their parents whilst at the same time enjoying the same freedom, *within the constraints they choose to impose on themselves*, which they see in the behaviour of their male peers as well as in their white friends.

Finally, it is worth bearing in mind that the right women to participate in sport and physical recreation, even in Western Europe, has a fairly short history. As McCrone (1987) wrote, it was the development of the girls' public schools that made possible the legitimation of physical exercise for women in the same way as they created middle-class women university students, doctors, politicians and the like. With that legitimation:

> . . . came recognition that women's limitations in sport have less to do with genetics than with the social and cultural codes that kept women alienated from their own bodies and protected the privileges and superiority of men.

In the light of the above, it seems reasonable to make the following observations.

- British law gives no support to men who seek to impose different moral or behavioural standards on women from those which they adopt for themselves. In the absence of a British 'Bill of Rights' the European Convention and the International Covenant (to both of which the United Kingdom is a contracting party) suggest the way that public policy is most likely to move. Although the law, through the process of judicial interpretation, allows for some accommodation to be made to the various ethnic origins, religions and customs of minority groups, it seems unlikely that it will give its support to practices arising from customs which deny rights to women within one group which are allowed to all others.
- From the early part of this century, British society has increasingly accepted that women have equal rights with men and should be afforded equal opportunities to pursue their ambitions within the law. This principle has been most recently enshrined in the Sex Discrimination Act of 1975.
- The findings of our study indicate that women from all ethnic groups would like to take a greater part in sport and physical recreation. They have many constraints in common but South Asian women generally and those of Pakistani and Bangladeshi origin in particular, suffer from the additional obstacles imposed by culture and custom and from a well-justified sense of physical insecurity if they are out of the home.
- Evidence from interview material and statistical data taken together suggest that South Asian women born in Britain or educated in British schools enjoyed their experience of school and, no less than their white, Chinese and Afro-Caribbean counterparts, they enjoyed their PE and games lessons there.
- Virtually all respondents said that the end of schooling meant a complete break with organized recreation. This accords perfectly with the generally accepted view of researchers and other commentators on the British education system. They find that there is a severe shortage of effective post-school provision *of and kind* for sixteen-year-old school leavers.
- In the light of the above, we would suggest that ethical objections, that might be made on the grounds of undue interference with long-held social and domestic practices, to the encouragement and provision of facilities for greater participation by women of South Asian origin are

outweighed by Britain's legal framework and the general thrust of public policy.

- Having reached this conclusion, the issue remains one of conflicting views and we would certainly not advocate a 'bull at the gate' approach to increasing their participation — not least because we do not believe it would work.

It might be argued that in a number of respects, the communities originating from South Asia were fortunate in bringing with them religions, cultures and customs that were of great antiquity and strongly held. Although they combined to distinguish them from the generality of British society, they also provided their adherents with powerful mechanisms with which to withstand assaults upon their self-image and self-respect by many of the institutions of British society and by white racists. As we have seen, however, whilst these mechanisms have served to protect these communities, they have also tended to isolate them from benefits as well as from harm.

In seeking to attract increasing numbers into participating in sport and leisure, the Sports Council and its many partners face notable problems. Strategies which have been successfully employed to increase participation by white British low- or non-participants — price reductions, more and better facilities, effective advertising campaigns and the like — will not, of themselves, be effective in attracting South Asian minority groups. These approaches will be effective only if they are part of an overall strategy which takes as its starting point the recognition that Britain is a multi-racial and a multi-cultural society. Such a recognition clears the way forward, justifies a proactive stance and sets the parameters within which action can sensibly be taken.

A dialogue has to be initiated and sustained with local minority groups by an increased range of providers, working in partnerships founded on common objectives with the Sports Council. This dialogue should have, as its first objective, the establishment of mutual understanding and trust between the providers and the communities. To be effective, it needs to be initiated and maintained at a range of levels. Certainly it needs to have a formal element, with representatives of the providers and the communities meeting at prescribed intervals with agreed agendas. However, we think it unlikely that, of themselves, such exchanges will be effective in leading to greater participation. We would attach much more importance to the work that needs to be done at the grassroots level by full-time, part-time and voluntary workers operating within a range of agencies. It is our opinion, supported by observation during the course of our research, that, all things being equal, these workers are more likely to achieve desired outcomes if they are of the same ethnicity as the community with which they are dealing and are preferably members of it. We highlight here the part that is being played by the Youth and Community Service and the education service. We would not wish to suggest that they are alone in having access to ethnic minority groups. We believe, however, that these services have a great deal to offer because, in the case of the education service, it is held in high esteem and those working in it are given considerable trust by parents. In the case of the Youth and Community Service, we were greatly impressed by the strategies it adopted in doing its work with ethnic minority youngsters and in its ability to integrate itself with those communities. Needless to say, both services have as their primary aim the life enhancement of their client groups.

It is difficult to over emphasize the importance that should be attached to this aim. Sport and physical recreation do not take place in a vacuum. For the participants it is a part of their lives which provides its own particular rewards but is none the less consistent with the general thrust of their culture. To put it another way, it is built in to their total perception of themselves and the society they live in and not something that has been simply bolted on as an optional extra.

To this has to be added the fact that these activities are firmly located in the mainstream provision designed to meet the needs and expectations of a white, liberal, essentially protestant society. It is self-evident that the ethnic minority groups living in Britain are not white, are not Christian and, in many cases, are profoundly distrustful of the morals and mores of British society. To this has to be added their experiences, either at first or second hand, of racism in its varied forms.

The dialogue should seek to discover the immediate felt needs of the community which would form the basis of short-term responses to satisfy them. At the same time it would form the opportunity to encourage the exploration by its members of ways to make it possible for non- and low- participants within it to raise their level of activity. As our findings demonstrate, women will form a large proportion of these groups and of these, Pakistani and Bangladeshi women are seen to be both the least participant whilst having expressed strong desires to do more. We are in no doubt that the local authorities and schools will have to bear the prime (virtually the exclusive) responsibility for meeting those needs. At a time when both local government and schools are in the process of rapid change, the leisure needs of ethnic minority groups require a powerful sponsor to ensure that their interests are not subordinated to more pressing and immediate concerns.

It might have been supposed that settlers from the Caribbean were fortunate by comparison with those from South Asia. They saw themselves as British citizens who happened to be black. Their religion, even if not strongly adhered to, where it existed at all was predominantly Christian and it generally informed their society. Their habits of thought were little different from those of their British peers and in their approach to work and recreation they owed much to British influence. Thus, on coming to Britain, they were ill-prepared for the kind of reception that awaited them — see, for instance, Carter, Harris and Joshi (1987) for the Government's response to the early black settlers from the Caribbean. They had none of the defensive options open to the South Asians who were to follow them. For them, the colour of their skins marked them out as objects of discrimination at all levels by people whom they perceived as being, in all essentials, similar to themselves. It was only with the rise of the Black

Power movement in the United States that they were provided with an adequate defence against the hostile social and economic environment in which they found themselves.

The results of our study appear to support the view that there is little difference between people of Caribbean origin and their indigenous white peers. Their religious affiliation, their notions of gender difference, their approach to leisure and the place and nature of sport and recreation within it were comparable. We suspect that the same might well be true of Caribbeans living in America.

It was not a primary intention of this study to reinforce the existing powerful evidence demonstrating the effects of racism on ethnic minority groups. The sense of rejection which it created in them, allied to housing practices adopted by public and private landlords which combined to form districts in which families of Caribbean origin predominated are well enough known. It is possible to distinguish the processes leading to the formation of such communities from those formed by those settlers from South India. As we have demonstrated, there were cultural and social forces which would, in any event, have made the formation of closely knit communities of Pakistanis, or Bangladeshis or Punjabis or other South Indian groups probable. There were no such forces acting on the settlers from the Caribbean. Inter-island differences are clearly perceived and powerfully felt by their inhabitants. Settlers from Jamaica would feel little affinity with others from Trinidad for example. The major cause of their present settlement patterns was, and remains, racial discrimination based on skin colour and reinforced by fears about economic competition on the part of the white working class. Thus, as Cashmore (1982) describes the maturing process of young blacks,

> The idea that they, as blacks, share a common destiny is a powerful one and social arrangements are organized accordingly. As Cyrille Regis put it, 'We, black kids, tended to drift away from white guys after school, or it may have been just before.' This results in a clustering together of black kids and initiates the process of what Mickey Morris calls 'learning to be black.'

He then argues that for young blacks, sport can provide a sense of identity and that success in it is a source of positive self-image. Thus, although success at the highest level is fraught with uncertainty, the barriers they see to other careers make even that uncertainty an attractive proposition. It may be that these factors account for the clearly articulated wish expressed by some members of the Caribbean community for the creation of facilities that would enable black people, particularly youngsters, to learn and practise their sports within the black community. In this way, they argued, they would at the same time acquire skills in their chosen sport *and* confidence in themselves and thus equip themselves better to progress both in their sport and in society generally.

It may be argued that such provision is inconsistent with the ideals of a free and equal society. However, we would suggest that the best way to make progress is to recognize the reality of a society that is *un*equal in the opportunities it offers and that those who suffer from structural inequality, suffer also from a reduction of freedom. We would further suggest that one way of making equality a reality is to take positive action in favour of those in most need and that this action should be designed to empower them in the pursuit of their goals. We would also add at this point that not all those interviewed pressed for provision uniquely for black youngsters. It was also suggested that the problem was two-fold: race and class. Those taking this line felt that there were many under-privileged white people who shared many of the disadvantages of their black peers, except, of course that of overt or covert racism. In their view, the solution was to be found in providing for all disadvantaged inner-urban people, who would benefit both from the provision and from mixing on equal terms in a recreational context (see Jarvie, 1991, for a more detailed discussion).

So what needs to be done? There are no easy answers to this question. There is no 'quick fix' of the kind beloved by politicians and managers everywhere. If sport and physical recreation is to be made more attractive and more accessible to people from ethnic minority groups, far-reaching strategies, applied through carefully developed policies and meticulously monitored to ensure their effective application must be employed. Furthermore, it has to be recognized that the desired outcomes will be slow; that the process will put demands on the leisure industry's resources; and that the benefits afforded to those groups whose opportunities have been restricted or denied may be at the expense of some of the privileges that have come to be regarded as 'rights' by the white majority.

On the other hand, the leisure industry is very large, highly profitable and can well afford to divert a tiny fraction of its resources to achieve the ends which we are advocating. Indeed, it might well wish to regard the exercise as an investment since the whole object is to increase participation by people who, at present, do little or nothing at all, but who *want* to do more. Moreover, the leisure industry is an interesting example of a hybrid made up of private and state investment.

We have emphasized the part played by local government in meeting the needs of the population generally through schools, leisure services departments and the Youth and Community Service. There are also the governing bodies which oversee and seek to extend the activities of the vast range of sporting and recreational activities in Britain. It is easy to assume that the resources to keep these sports in business are raised through club subscriptions, gate receipts and sponsorship. Even here, however, the state makes substantial contributions through such bodies as the Sports Council, as well as through direct support in the name of national benefit as, for example, in backing Manchester's Olympic bid. The state exhibits a lively interest in sport at elite levels. As Hargreaves (1986) wrote:

> Above all, it is the great national and international sporting occasions, constructed nowadays for the nation by the mass media, that provide some of the most powerful images of national unity today. Such occasions celebrate and identify a popular activity with the way of life of a

nation, but the symbolic work carried out with the aid of national flags, the parades, the uniforms, the team colours, the martial music, the hymns and the national anthem, the opening and closing ceremonies (especially the award ceremonies) represents the dominant group's cultural capital being put to work to hegemonize the spectacle. (Hargreaves, 1986)

It is not altogether surprising that the country's political elite are present on these occasions. However, in the context of many of the ethnic minority groups, such events do not provide images of 'national unity' because they cannot identify with them through their own experience. Far from being a shared, unifying image, they are for many, a symbol of the disunity they feel.

The Sports Council, the governing bodies of sport, local authority and commercial providers should review their employment policies and procedures and set targets for the employment of people from ethnic minorities. These targets should specify the numbers and proportions of ethnic minority people and should be established for every grade of appointment within the organization, together with realistic timescales for their achievement. In conjunction with this, monitoring systems should be put in place so as to measure progress towards the goals of equality of opportunity in employment.

There has to be a recognition by all providers of the complexity of settlement patterns of ethnic minority groups and the variations in their religious, social and cultural imperatives. This means that a successful venture in one town or city cannot necessarily be replicated in another. Appropriate action can only be arrived at as a result of consultation between the providers and the communities, and the consultation must be genuine. As long ago as 1985 the Commission for Racial Equality warned of the existence of phony consultation processes.

The communities felt that what the [local authority] councils meant by consultation was not a matter of getting the views of the communities and acting upon them, but rather a means of telling the communities what was going to be done regardless. (Commission for Racial Equality, 1985)

Genuine consultation is not simply our exchange of views between two or more parties, one of which is likely, in the nature of things, to be in a more powerful position than the other. It is rather a process by which the parties concerned seek to learn more about each other; to understand the motives which underlie each other's responses to developing situations and recognize the limitations — cultural, legal, financial, whatever they may be — which define the boundaries of the possible for both sides.

Consultation processes of this kind are both time consuming and long term but the rewards are greater than a good outcome as measured by the cost-effectiveness of the venture being discussed. A constant refrain in earlier chapters was of the need to develop trust between parties, and of the distrust which existed in the minds of many of the ethnic minority groups towards white society generally. 'Distrust' is not being used here in the context of racism and the very understandable fears people from ethnic minorities have of its various manifes-tations. Rather, we are referring to a distrust of many of the characteristics of British society about which it prides itself — characteristics such as personal liberty, the independence of children and young people, religious freedom, the distinction between morality and the law, all those characteristics which go to distinguish an essentially protestant Christian society from what has been described as the 'collectivist' societies of many ethnic minority communities. And, of course, the traffic will not be all one way. Much will be learned by the white British, leading to a reduction of suspicion and an increased respect for values that were previously imperfectly understood.

Given this kind of consultation process, many of the problems facing man-agers in local authorities, the Sports Council and others in the leisure industry, will, if not evaporate, at least change into other, less intractable problems. Thus, for example, the decision whether or not it is necessary or beneficial to make special provision for South Asian women and, if so, what should it be, will be resolved in the consultation process. In fact, the process will probably result in changes of position on both sides. Once, however, a solution acceptable to both sides is arrived at, the managers are faced with residual problems — cost, social and political acceptance — which they are (or should be) well able to handle.

Much could be done to increase participation at little cost. The work of the Youth and Community Service with youngsters from all ethnic groups was very impressive and most of it was being done on a shoestring. They succeeded because they were constantly negotiating with the groups who formed their clientele. Nor did they seem in the least dismayed at making special provision for groups with particular needs.

The Sports Council exerts an influence out of all proportion to its size and financial resources as a result of its strategy of working in partnership with all the major providers. It is held in high regard by them for its commitment and for the expertize and enthusiasm of its officers. It is therefore uniquely placed to exert its influence on virtually all voluntary and statutory bodies involved in the provi-sion of sport and physical recreation. Through its partnerships it can give pow-erful encouragement to providers by making it a condition of its continued support that they recognize the needs of ethnic minority groups and demonstrate their intentions to meet those needs. The result will not only be an increase in par-ticipation but a society that has been made a little more just, fairer and more harmonious. Attempting to attain the goals of pluralism, sport and recreation in twenty-first century Europe.

As we have hinted before, sport and politics are now inextricably entwined. This view is often irritably rejected by many participants but its truth is inescapable (see, most recently, Coghlan, 1990). In the light of information provided by the 1991 census reported by Ballard and Kalra (1994), it would be well if politicians and sports providers seriously addressed the needs of minority communities. Their children already constitute nearly 9 per cent of the pre-school age group. It would be an act of political and sporting folly if the needs of these youngsters were to be ignored.

Bibliography

ABERCROMBIE, N., WADE, A., SOOTHILL, K., URRY, J. and WALBY, S. (1988) *Contemporary British Society*, Polity Press.

AIREY, C. and BROOK, L. (1986) *British Social Attitudes, the 1986 Report*, England, Gower Publishing.

ALAM, F. (1988) *The Salience of Homeland*, Research Papers in Ethnic Relations No. 7, Centre for Research in Ethnic Relations, University of Warwick.

ALLISON, M. (1988) *Breaking Boundaries and Barriers: Future Directions in Cross-Cultural Research*, London, Taylor and Francis.

BACHU, P. (1985) *Twice Migrants: East African Sikh Settlers in Britain*, Tavistock.

BACHU, P. (1985) *Parental Educational Strategies: The Case of the Punjabi Sikhs in Britain*, Research Papers in Ethnic Relations No.3, Centre for Research in Ethnic Relations, University of Warwick.

BAGLEY, C. (1977) *A Comparative Perspective on the Education of Black Children in Britain*, Paper presented at the University of Manchester.

BAKER, H. (1981) *Teaching Chinese Children: A Teacher's Guide*, London, Nuffield Foundation.

BALLARD, R. (1989) *The Sikh Diaspora: Differentiation and Disjunction Amongst the Sikhs in Britain*, Delhi.

BALLARD, R. (1990) 'Migration and kinship: The differential effect of marriage rules on the processes of Punjabi migration to Britain', in CLARKE, C. *South Asians Overseas*, Cambridge University Press.

BALLARD, R. and KALRA, V.S. (1994) *The Ethnic Dimensions of the 1991 Census-A Preliminary Report*, Census Microdata Unit, Manchester, University of Manchester.

BASHAM, A. (1959) (Ed.) *Hinduism* in ZAEHNER, R. *Concise Encyclopedia of Living Faiths*, London, Hutchinson.

BAYLISS, T. (1989) 'PE and racism: Making changes', *Multicultural Teaching*, **7**,2, pp. 19–22.

BOTHOLO *et al.* (1986) *A Sporting Chance*, The work of the Greater London Council Sports Sub-Committee 1983–1985 and a Review of the Brixton Recreation Centre, Greater London Council.

BOURDIEU, P. (1974) 'The school as a conservative force: Scholastic and cultural inequalities', in EGGLESTON, S. (Ed.) *Contemporary Research in the Sociology of Education*, London, Methuen.

BOYLE, R.H. (1971) 'Negroes in baseball', in DUNNING, E. (Ed.) *The Sociology of Sport*, London, Frank Cass.

BROOKS, D. and SINGH, K. (1978/79) 'Ethnic commitment versus structural reality: South Asian immigrant workers in Britain', *New Community*, **7**,1.

CARRINGTON, B., CHIVERS, T. and WILLIAMS, T. (1987) 'Gender, leisure and sport: A case study of young people of south Asian descent', *Leisure Studies*, **6**,3, pp. 265–79.

CARRINGTON, B. and WILLIAMS, T. (1988) 'Patriarchy and ethnicity: The link between school, physical education and community leisure activities', in EVANS, J. (Ed.) *Teachers, Teaching and Control in Physical Education*, London, Falmer Press.

CARRINGTON, E. and WOOD, E. (1983) 'Body-talk: Images of sport in a multiracial school', *Multiracial Education*, **11**,2, pp. 29–38.

CARROLL, R. and HOKLLINSHEAD, G. (1990) 'Ethnicity and conflict in physical education', in JARVIE, G. (Ed.) *Ethnicity, Racism and Sport*, London, Falmer Press.

CARTER, B., HARRIS, C. and JOSHI, S. (1987) *The 1951–55 Conservative Government and the Racialisation of Black Immigration*, Policy Papers in Ethnic Relations, No. 11. Centre for Research in Ethnic Relations, University of Warwick.

CASHMORE, E. (1982) *Black Sportsmen*, London, Routledge and Kegan Paul.

CASHMORE, E. (1982a) 'Black youth, sport and education', *New Community*, Vol. **X**,2, pp. 213–21.

CLARK, E. (1957) *My Mother who Fathered Me*, London, Allen and Unwin.

CLOUGH, H. and QUARMBY, J. (1978) *A Public Library Service for Ethnic Minorities in Great Britain*, London, The Library Association.

COGHLAN, J.F. with WEBB, I.M. (1990) *Sport and British Politics since 1960*, London, Falmer Press.

COMMISSION FOR RACIAL EQUALITY, (1983) *Positive Action and Equal Opportunity in Employment*, London, CRE.

COMMISSION FOR RACIAL EQUALITY, (1985) *Review of the Race Relations Act 1976: Proposals for Change*, London, CRE.

COMMISSION FOR RACIAL EQUALITY, (1985) *Towards Genuine Consultation: Principles of Community Participation*, London, CRE.

DES, (1983) *Young People in the 80s: A Survey*, London, HMSO.

DIXEY, R. (1982) 'Asian women and sport — the Bradford experience', *British Journal of Physical Education*, **13**,4, pp. 108–14.

EDWARDS, H. (1970) *The Revolt of the Black Athlete*, New York, Free Press.

EDWARDS, H. (1973) *Sociology of Sport*, Illinois, Dorsey.

EQUAL OPPORTUNITIES WORKING PARTY, First Report (1986).

FLEMING, S. (1989) *Sport and Asian Youth Culture*, Paper at a British Sociological Association Workshop, Sport and Ethnicity, University of Warwick.

FOSTER, P. (1990) *Policy and Practice in Multicultural and Anti-Racist Education*, London, Routledge.

GARVEY, A. and JACKSON, B. (1975) *Chinese Children*, Windsor, NFER.

GHAI, D.P. (1965) *Portrait of a Minority: Asians in East Africa*, Oxford, Oxford University Press.

GHUMAN, P. (1991) *Best or Worst of Two Worlds: A Study of Asian Adolescents*, Windsor, NFER.

GREATER LONDON COUNCIL, (1983) *Sport and Recreation Management — Positive Action Training Programme for Ethnic Minorities*, Report to the GLTB, Arts and Recreation and Ethnic Minorities Committee, Greater London Council.

GREER, G. (1984) *Sex and Destiny: Politics of Human Fertility*, Picador.

GRIFFITH, M. (1987) 'Physical education in one multicultural society?', *Bulletin of Physical Education*, **23**,1, pp. 45–6.

GUTMANN (1978) *From Ritual to Record*, New York.

HAMMOND, P. (1990) *Manchester Schools Language Survey 1990*, Final Report, Manchester City Council Education Department.

HARGREAVES, J. (1986) *Sport, Power and Culture*, Cambridge, Polity Press.

HARGREAVES, J. (1986) 'The state and sport' in ALLISON, L. (Ed.) *The Politics of Sport*, Manchester, University of Manchester.

HINNELLS, J.R. and SHARPE, E.J. (1972) (Eds) *Hinduism*, England, Oriel Press.

HMSO (1988) Local Government (2) Act.

HMSO (1989) *Social Trends*, from Central Statistical Office, London, HMSO.

HOCH, P. (1974) 'The battle over racism', in SAGE, G.H. (Ed.) *Sport and American Society*, Selected Readings, 2nd Edition, Reading, Mass, Addison Wesley.

HONG KONG GOVERNMENT INFORMATION SERVICES, (1984) *Hong Kong: The Facts, Religion and Custom*, Hong Kong, Government Printer.

IKULAYO, P.B. (1978) 'Ethnic background, physical ability and attitude towards PE amongst 13 year old girls in a London Comprehensive School', Unpublished M.Ed Dissertation, University of Manchester.

JARVIE, G. (1991) (Ed.) *Sport, Racism and Ethnicity*, London, Falmer Press.

KANE, M. (1971) 'An assessment of black is best', *Sports Illustrated*, **34**,3, pp. 78–83.

KARN, V. (1983) 'Race and housing in Britain: The role of major institutions', in GLAZER, N. and YOUNG, K. (Eds), *Ethnic Pluralism and Public Policy*, Lexington Books, Toronto.

KEW, S. (1979) *Ethnic Groups and Leisure*, A Review for the Joint Panel on Leisure and Recreation Research, London, Sports Council.

KING, P., TOWN, S. and WARNER, S. (1983) *Leisure Provision and Ethnic Minorities in Bradford* in LSA Newsletter Supplement, 11–22, LSA.

LADLOW, D. (undated), *Aspects of Chinese Culture*, mimeograph, Crown St., Language Centre, Liverpool.

LEWIS, T. (1979) *Ethnic Influences on Girls' PE*, B.J.P.E., 105, 132.

MCCRONE, K.M. (1987) 'Sport and the Late-Victorian public school', in MANGAN, J.A. and PARK, R.J. (Eds) *From Fair Sex to Feminism: Sport and the Socialisation of Women in the Industrial and Post-Industrial Eras*, London.

McLeod, W.H. (1976) *The Evolution of the Sikh Community*, Oxford.

Miller, D. (1985) *First Class Athletes, Second Class Citizens*, London, *The Times*, 16 August, p. 8.

Modgil, S. *et al.* (1986) *Multicultural Education: The Interminable Debate*, London, Falmer Press.

Nehru, J. (1961) *The Discovery of India*, New York, Doubleday.

Ng, Kwee Choo, (1968) *The Chinese in London*, Oxford, Oxford University Press.

North-West Region of the Sports Council, (1990) in Fact File No.1.

Oldham Metropolitan Borough Council (1990) Research Section, *Interim Report of the 1989 Census of Bangladeshis in Oldham*, Oldham MBC.

Ouseley, H. (1983) *London Against Racism in Sport and Recreation*, Report of a Seminar, Sport and Recreation in London's Inner City, 14–20, Greater London Council.

Parekh, B. (1989) *Identities on Parade*, Marxism Today, June.

Pettigrew, J. (1972) *Some Notes on the Social System of the Sikh Jats*, New Community.

Pitt, P. (1983) *Scarman and After: The Greater London Council Response*, in LSA Newsletter Supplement, 3–10, LSA.

Poulter, S. (1989) 'The claim to a separate Islamic system of personal law for British Muslims', in Mallat, C. and Connors, J. (Eds) *Islamic Family Law*, Graham and Trotman.

Poulter, S. (1990) 'Cultural pluralism and its limits: A legal perspective' in *Britain: A Plural Society*, Report of a Seminar, London, Commission for Racial Equality.

Radhakrishnan, S. (1971) *The Hindu View of Life*, London, Unwin Books, 16th Impression.

Raval, S. (1989) 'Gender, leisure and sport: A case study of young people of south Asian descent, a response', *Leisure Studies*, **8**, pp. 237–40.

Rex, J. and Tomlinson, S. (1979) *Colonial Immigration in a British City*, London, Routledge and Kegan Paul.

Scarman, Lord. (1982) *The Brixton Disorders, 10–12 April 1981*, Penguin Books.

Simsova, S. and Chinn, W. (1982) *Library Needs of Chinese in London*, School of Librarianship and Information Studies, Polytechnic of North London.

Smith, D.J. and Tomlinson, S. (1989) *The School Effect*, London, Policy Studies Institute.

Snyder, E.E. and Spreitzer, E.A. (1983) 'The black athlete' in *Social Aspect of Sport*, Prentice Hall.

Spink, J. (1989) 'Urban development, leisure facilities and the inner city', in Branham, P., Henry, I., Mommas, H. and Van Der Poel, H. (Eds) *Leisure and Urban Processes*, Routledge.

Sports Council (1988) *Into the 90s: A Strategy for Sport, 1988–1993*, London, Sports Council.

Sports Council (1990) *Recruitment Policy and Procedures*, London, Sports Council.

Swann Report (1985) *Education For All*, The report of the Committee of Inquiry into the Education of Children from Ethnic Minority Groups. Chairman: Lord Swann. London, HMSO.

TAYLOR, M. (1981) *Caught Between*, Windsor, NFER-Nelson.

TAYLOR, M. (1987) *Chinese Pupils in Britain*, Windsor, NFER-Nelson.

TIERNEY, J. (1982) (Ed.) *Race, Migration and Schooling*, London, Holt, Rinehart and Winston.

TINKER, H. (1977) *Race, Conflict and the International Order*, London, Macmillan.

TOMLINSON, S. and SMITH, D.J. (1989) *The School Effect: A Study of Multicultural Comprehensives*, London, Policy Studies Institute.

TROYNA, B. and BALL, W. (1984) 'Multi-cultural education: Policy in practice' in *Race and Immigration*, London, Runnymede Trust.

TROYNA, B. and WILLIAMS, J. (1986) *Racism, Education and the State*, London, Croom Helm.

ULLAH, P. and BROTHERTON, C. (1989) 'Sex, social class and ethnic differences in the expectations of unemployment and psychological well-being of secondary school pupils in England' in *British Journal of Educational Psychology*, Vol. **59**, Part 1.

VERMA, G.K. (1986) *Ethnicity and Educational Achievement*, London, Macmillan.

VERMA, G.K. (1989) *Education for All: A Landmark in Pluralism*, London, Falmer Press.

VERMA, G.K. and DARBY, D. (1987) *Race, Training and Employment*, London, Falmer Press.

VERMA, G.K. and MALLICK, K. (1981) 'Hinduism and multicultural education', in LYNCH, J. (Ed.) *Teaching in the Multi-Cultural School*, London, Ward Lock Educational.

VERMA, G.K. and PUMFREY, P. (1988) *Educational Attainments: Issues and Outcomes in Multicultural Education*, London, Falmer Press.

WALVIN, J. (1984) *Passage To Britain*, Penguin Books.

WEINREICH, P. and KELLY, A.J.D. (1990) 'Collectivism and Individualism in Identity Development: Muslim British and Anglo-Saxon British Identities', paper given at International Conference, *Individualism and Collectivism: Psychological Perspective from East and West*, Seoul, Korean Psychological Association.

WHEELER, H. (1966) *Civilisations of the Indus Valley and Beyond*, London, Thames and Hudson.

WHEELER, H. (1968) *The Indus Civilisation*, Cambridge, Cambridge University Press.

WOOD, E.R. and CARRINGTON, L.B. (1982) 'School, sport and the black athlete', *Physical Education Review*, **5**,2, pp. 131–7.

Index